Co-Parenting after Divorcing a Narcissist

A Divorce Recovery Guide to Bouncing Back After A Toxic Relationship of Emotional and Narcissistic Abuse with Co-Parenting Tips to Disarm and Protect

Isabella Francis

© Copyright 2022 - All rights reserved.

The content contained within this book may not be reproduced, duplicated or transmitted without direct written permission from the author or the publisher.

Under no circumstances will any blame or legal responsibility be held against the publisher, or author, for any damages, reparation, or monetary loss due to the information contained within this book, either directly or indirectly.

Legal Notice:

This book is copyright protected. It is only for personal use. You cannot amend, distribute, sell, use, quote or paraphrase any part, or the content within this book, without the consent of the author or publisher.

Disclaimer Notice:

Please note the information contained within this document is for educational and entertainment purposes only. All effort has been executed to present accurate, up to date, reliable, complete information. No warranties of any kind are declared or implied.

Readers acknowledge that the author is not engaged in the rendering of legal, financial, medical or professional advice. The content within this book has been derived from various sources. Please consult a licensed professional before attempting any techniques outlined in this book.

By reading this document, the reader agrees that under no circumstances is the author responsible for any losses, direct or indirect, that are incurred as a result of the use of the information contained within this document, including, but not limited to, errors, omissions, or inaccuracies.

Table of Contents

Introduction	1
Part One: Divorce Aftermath	5
Chapter One: Let Yourself Grieve	6
Focus: It is okay to grieve your marriage.	6
Now I'm divorced, what next?	8
Financial Survival Checklist before the divorce	10
Financial Survival Checklist during the divorce	18
Why am I finding it hard to move on?	27
Is Divorce Grief Real?	29
Phases in divorce recovery	31
The Stages of Divorce	32
How long does it take to heal from a divorce?	34
Steps to moving on after divorce	37
Chapter Two: The After-Effects Of Narcissistic Abuse	43
Was it truly a toxic relationship?	45
Can You Experience PTSD From Being With a Narcissistic Partner	50

Examining Narcissistic Victim Syndrome (NVS)   56

Does Positive Psychology Help?   63

Safeguarding yourself after divorcing a narcissist   71

Chapter Three: Clearing The Mess After   79

What to do When Your Friends and Family Are Not Being Supportive   81

Handling the Gossip and Disapproving looks   84

Handling Debts and Finances After   89

Part Two: Protecting Yourself And Your Child   93

Chapter Four: Helping Your Children Come to Terms with Things   95

Your Child Was Hurt Too   97

Helping Your Child Handle the Divorce News   99

How To Discuss Your Divorce With Your Kids   101

Teenagers   104

Common Questions Your Kids are Likely to Ask (And Appropriate Answers to Give)   107

Helping Your Kids Heal From the Emotional Abuse You All Went Through   109

When Your Child is Experiencing Loyalty Conflicts   112

How Loyalty Conflicts Can Impact Your Child   114

Is Therapy Necessary For The Kid?   117

Chapter Five: Disarming The Narcissist   120

The Psychology of the Narcissist   121

Setting Boundaries With a Narcissist   125

How to Keep Calm When They are Infuriating   130

Table of Contents

Arming Yourself Against The Narcissist … 132

Stand Up for Yourself and Stop People-pleasing … 135

Protecting Your Child Against the Narcissist's Tactics and Abuse … 138

Chapter Six: Co-Parenting With The Narcissist Ex … 142

Co-parenting With a Narcissist is Challenging … 143

What to Expect When Co-parenting … 145

Parental Alienation is a Thing … 147

How Parents Cause Loyalty Conflict … 151

When To Choose Parallel Parenting Instead … 152

Part Three: Moving On With Grace … 154

Chapter Seven: Positive Co-Parenting: How To … 156

The Concept of Positive Parenting … 157

Improving Your Relationship With Your Child … 159

Strategies For Positive Co-Parenting … 163

Why Positive Co-Parenting Is Important … 167

Helping Your Kids Develop Mental Resilience … 170

Chapter Eight: Rebuilding Your Life … 173

Take Your Time: Don't Rush Things … 174

Self-care is Important … 174

Making New Friends … 177

Reinventing Yourself … 180

Taking Time to do Things You and Your Child Enjoy … 182

Joining Support Groups … 184

You Can Love Again … 186

Conclusion 188

References 191

Introduction

You're probably not prepared for this part. I mean, sure you may have heard that divorces aren't a walk in the park and can drain your lifeblood. Fair enough. You may have consulted a good divorce lawyer who walked you through all the steps. You may even have gotten a mediator to try to resolve issues peacefully. By all standards, you may even have had a 'successful divorce.'

Or it may have been a messy process for you and everyone else involved. Perhaps you didn't even have a good support system during the divorce. You had to rough it out by yourself and stay strong for your kids. You've had to take several deep breaths, cups of coffee, and a few power naps to stay sane. You had to keep on moving, no matter what.

I know, everyone says that the worst is over now that the divorce is done. Maybe you even thought you were home free after it. You probably didn't realize that the hardest part starts after the divorce. You probably didn't think you'd have to keep fighting so damn hard after surviving the divorce. You definitely were not ready for this part. This one important part of your marriage that still needs to stay safe. Your kids. But before we discuss them, let's look at you.

Divorcing a narcissist is just one step of the journey. You may find it hard to move on from your marriage. Once again, you realize that it was a toxic situation and hellish for the kids. But a part of you yearns for the way things were before, the rare, good moments when you felt like a real family. A part of you may want your kids to have both of their parents together, or you just haven't accepted the reality of your split. That's perfectly normal.

Here's something that a lot of newly divorced partners refuse to accept: narcissistic abuse will scar you. The effects of this toxic relationship will linger and change you. It doesn't matter if you think you've escaped or you're 'fine'; the odds are that you're most certainly not fine. Most survivors of narcissistic abuse often experience Post Traumatic Stress Disorder (PTSD). The truth is denial will only hinder your healing.

If you're 'trying to be strong' for your kids, guess what? Your kids need the honest, unfettered version of you right now. They need to see you as a safe space to express their vulnerabilities. I hate t0 sound cliche, but you can't help your kids heal if you haven't healed yourself. So what's the easiest way to heal from narcissistic abuse? What's the most straightforward, no-bullshit path to help you bounce back? You need a guide to show you practical tips for moving on after a divorce. You need to understand why you're feeling stuck and how to sort out your finances now that you're divorced; heck, you need to prepare yourself for possible disagreements and disapproval from various quarters. You need a book that's honest enough to show you how it is and how to flourish, regardless.

Let's get real; your kids need to learn how to get through this divorce. They need all the help they can get from you. How will they relate with your narcissist co-parent? How can they survive this ordeal unscathed? What will you do if your ex is being uncooperative? What are the odds they'll stop being their manipulative, emotionally abusive self after the divorce? I gotta tell you; they are slim to none. Do you think they'll suddenly become model parents after a divorce? Sure, they might have fooled the court, but you know the truth. How will your children survive being parented by such a toxic person? Can their mental health handle it? How can you and they, by extension, learn to disarm the narcissist? Can your kids become resilient even in the face of all that toxicity? Can they learn how to process their feelings and communicate them to you instead of acting out?

Look, I know exactly how this could make you feel. I guess you could say that I'm extremely passionate about the intersection where positive co-parenting meets recovering from narcissistic abuse. I've studied the best positive co-parenting techniques that help you cope with a narcissistic co-parent. What's more, I've helped several people apply these principles with remarkable success.

Achieving freedom from emotional abuse is something I had to fight tooth and nail for. I learned to overcome my struggles with healing, finding, and loving my true self after narcissistic abuse. I had to dig deep to find the right moves to help you move on after a really tough divorce. I'm excited to announce that these strategies work.

I know. That's a very bold claim, but I can back it up. I've been able to apply different strategies. Some were not so rosy; others were screaming successes. One thing about the techniques you'll learn in this book is that they are practical, tested, and trusted. They are simple to understand, perfect for beginners, and still appropriate for those with a bit of narcissism experience. The bottom line is that I'm here to show you how to get where you need to be. How to be that parent that has successfully dealt with the trauma of narcissistic abuse, has healed themselves, and can hold their own against their narcissistic co-parent. That parent has successfully learnt how to regulate their emotions, has taught their children how to handle their narcissist parents, how to shine despite it all, and how to communicate productively instead of turning to alcohol or other dangerous habits. That parent lives a drama-free life, and they've learned how to disarm their narcissistic ex. They no longer cringe when they think of their kids spending weekends with the other parent, nor are they apprehensive at the sight of their ex. That parent sounds like you. This book is designed to help you become that person.

I don't know about you, but I'm a sucker for taking action instead of dwelling on what-ifs or maybes. That's why I think you should jump right into the next section and see why it's okay to grieve your lost marriage.

Part One

Divorce Aftermath

Chapter One

Let Yourself Grieve

Focus: It is okay to grieve your marriage.

"The narcissist is like a bucket with a hole in the bottom: No matter how much you put in, you can never fill it up. The phrase "I never feel like I am enough" is the mantra of the person in a narcissistic relationship. That's because to your narcissistic partner, you are not. No one is. Nothing is."– Ramani Durvasula

I once received a frantic message from Steve, one of my very good friends who was going through a divorce. He and Melanie, his wife, were set to part ways. After a long and stressful union, Steve finally summoned the courage to serve his wife with divorce papers. He knew it was a tricky thing to achieve. Of course, his lawyer had already told him that most women get full custody of their kids unless they were proven unfit to work or care for them. Steve was worried that he'd lose custody to his wife, but he also knew something other people didn't know. He knew his wife was a narcissist. She was obsessed with maintaining her sterling reputation and looking good to the world. His kids were slowly becoming withdrawn and uncommunicative whenever she was around. He knew he had to do something; for himself and his kids.

After a long and difficult court battle, he was able to win partial custody and visitation rights with his kids, thanks to his superstar lawyer. But he wasn't ready for what came next.

Let Yourself Grieve

"I knew she was a toxic parent, but I didn't realize that she'd become practically worse overnight. She was always trying to drop by the house unannounced, and she tried to extend her time with the kids whenever they were with her. She took a lot of surprise trips when the kids were with her; she didn't care that they were missing school or didn't even want to be around her. She was always arguing with me and trying to bait me into missing child support checks. When she noticed I was getting close to a lady friend, she turned up in unpleasant ways to cause a scene.

"The crazy part is that even after all these stunts she pulled, I still missed her. I found myself mourning our marriage, thinking of the good times. I started to wonder if she was really all that bad while we were married. I told myself that she only acted out because she didn't want this divorce. Maybe if we got back together and the kids had their mother back, everything would be fine. Looking back at it now, I didn't even realize that I hadn't gotten over her abusive actions and I'd created a trauma bond with her. I feel so stuck and so helpless. How can I break free from her? How can I save my kids? How can I be happy again? Am I going to live the rest of my life with her weight around my neck? I don't even know what I need, but I know I need help. For myself, for my kids. " -Steve

So many people are in Steve's shoes today and don't know what to do. They keep floundering around, trying to survive the day and losing each battle. What you don't know is that you can't win the war if you keep losing every battle. You can't keep brushing over your feelings and trying to push them away. You can't keep allowing other people's opinions and expectations to be your blueprint.

You need to wake up and step back into your life. You need to consider your kids and take stock of your situation and plan. You need to be like that brave, young general in *Mulan* that led his motley crew to victory. But you can't be victorious without a plan, a battle strategy if you will. You can't make a plan without assessing your situation and being honest about what gives.

Remember, you're not just doing this for yourself; you're doing this for your children, and they deserve the best, every time. You need to wake up!

Now I'm divorced, what next?

A lot of new divorcees are surprised and almost always look guilty when I tell them that it's OK to feel a little lost after their divorce. They perk up when I tell them it's very common to feel like you've been cast adrift after a fresh divorce. Even if you're the one that pushed for it.

I think the sooner you accept that life after a divorce can be the pits, the faster you can adjust to it. Instead of spending all that time floating along in the sea of The Nile (denial, see what I did there?), let's hasten to the shores of acceptance and find our way up the mountain of survival.

As always, I have to say that your survival in this period depends largely on you. You could turn this harrowing part of your life into a long-term reward for yourself. Or it could end up being the most miserable time of your life that you may never recover from. You could come away from this experience with positivity, peace, and happiness, or it could be a messy affair that damages you and affects everyone around you negatively. You could wear the proof of your experience with pride like a brave soldier, or you could hobble along, forever disabled by this experience.

I know what you're asking (and truth be told, you do too); yes, it is entirely possible to be happy after your divorce. It is possible to become that person with all the peace and contentment the world has to offer. It could be you telling other people that *"my divorce changed my life for the better and made me the happiest I've ever been,"* like Catrina, a dear lady I was fortunate to counsel, who shared this testimony with me after applying the strategies I'll tell you about in this book.

Yes. Yes, to everything. Yes, to your secret hopes and desires for true happiness. Yes, to living a life without further emotional damage but with full responsibility and strength going forward. Yes, to being the best parent for your kids, knowing that they feel safe and loved by you and can trust you with their emotions. Yes, to healthy, mentally balanced kids who don't develop a drug problem or become difficult simply because of the pressures of the divorce. The answer is yes. You can achieve it. The ball is in your court. If you play it right, you'll get to where you need to be. And I'll be with you every step of the way.

You can't control what your ex does or says. You can't decide what your kids feel at every point in time. You may not even be able to control your emotions, but guess what? You can control your responses. You can take charge of your actions carefully and decide how you'll behave. That right there is the key to your victory.

Now, let's get into the nitty-gritty. What next steps do you need to take now that you're divorced? Many people have different opinions about this, but I'll tell you the three key areas you need to look at, and quickly too. Your money, your personal life, and your legal affairs. Sounds like a no-brainer, right? Yet, you'd be shocked to find out that most newly divorced people don't pay special attention to these areas and end up suffering.

In the sea of confusion and amidst all the noise you're probably experiencing, here's what you should do:

Focus on the money

A study of common reasons for divorce among couples found that financial issues made up a remarkable 36.7% of the reason for divorce (Scott, 2013). Another study concluded that finances were responsible for 40% of divorces (Hawkins, 2012). In general, divorce is harsher on a woman's finances than on a man's. A study by the US Accountability office showed that women's household income was reduced by as much as 41% after divorcing past the age of 50. In general, separated women are more likely to fall into poverty than men (AACFL, 2022). Other studies among women in the US show a decline in income of 25% (Hauser, 2018) and 30% (de Vaus, 2017). As for men, it has been found that their income actually rises in the years after the divorce (AACFL, 2022).

No matter how you might spin it, money is important. It's an important factor for marriage, and it's important for divorce as well. Now that you're newly divorced, your major money focus should be on deciding your financial goals, being fiscally accountable, and tidying up any loose ends with your ex.

If you didn't sort out the finances during the divorce proceedings, this is a great time to do some basic financial decluttering.

Here's a basic financial survival checklist that has been helpful to a lot of people. I have to state here that there's no one-size-fits-all approach to money concerning a divorce. I know full well that your financial situation may be radically different from the next person's, so I recommend that you consult a divorce attorney licensed to practice in your state if you're unsure about something. Now that we have that out of the way, here's how to get started.

Financial Survival Checklist before the divorce

It's best to start organizing your finances before the divorce. If you suspect that a divorce is coming or you're the one initiating the divorce, you need to start thinking about your future financially and prepare. To this end:

Let Yourself Grieve

- Educate yourself about your financial status.

- If you don't know much about finances, as may be expected with a toxic partner, do some snooping around. Check the house for account statements or tax returns and make a copy for yourself.

- Which funds will you be able to access once the divorce is announced? How much do you have in your checking accounts or as cash at hand? Take stock of that and see if that's enough for you to live by as well as for your children. Do you have enough to retain the services of a good divorce attorney and other related needs? Try to start putting it aside. If the divorce is amicable, you can both agree on spending limits and savings. Or you can opt for an uncontested divorce where you don't have to hire a cutthroat attorney or take each other to the cleaners. You can jointly decide the terms of the divorce without going to court. If it's not amicable, ask about legal separation, which can help you get better access to the money until the divorce is done.

- Take note of your expenses and plan for future expenses. These records will help your attorney and the judge decide how the assets and debts will be split. It's also a huge determinant as to whether spousal support is to be awarded as well as its likely amount. The table below should help.

Current expenses	Future expenses
Utility bills	College tuition fund (if applicable)
Food	Instead of paying for child care, you may need to look at after-school activities as your child grows older,

	like junior league
Clothing	As your child develops their interests, things like piano lessons, ballet classes, etc., become necessary
Entertainment	Car insurance for the kids
Home maintenance	Instead of family vacations, summer camp for the kids may be an expense to plan for
Childcare	
Transportation	
Vacations	
Infrequent expenses like replacing the dryer or dishwasher.	

- Document your finances as much as possible.

This can be very time-consuming, so start as soon as possible. It may be best to do this on the down-low but note that any requests you make on a joint account will not be confidential. You should have this handy when it's time to meet your divorce attorney and your divorce financial analyst (if you choose to get one). Check out this table below to see what pertains to you.

Important financial records	Details and actions required
A list of assets and how much they are worth. Also, note their appreciation or depreciation value. Also, note which ones were brought into the marriage and those that have accumulated since marriage. Sometimes, you may need to determine the exact value of your assets; in this case, don't hesitate to get an appraisal done by a professional.	This includes anything that has a monetary value like

Cash at hand, cash in your checking accounts or savings account. Cash equivalents like certificates of deposit also count here.

Physical assets like your business, your property, art, jewelry, your car and stuff like that.

Intangible assets like stocks, pensions, royalties and bonds.

Liquid assets are things that can easily be converted to cash, like some types of stocks and bonds.

Fixed-income assets have fixed interest rates or dividends. They include securities, government bonds, money market funds, commercial paper, and certificates of |

	deposit, among others.
	Fixed assets. Also known as illiquid assets, they aren't easily converted to cash. They include furniture, antiques, real estate, etc.
A list of debts	This is basically any money owed in one form or another.
	Secured debts are those debts that have collateral in place. A good example is a car loan or even your mortgage. So, these assets get seized if your debt isn't repaid as agreed.
	Unsecured debt isn't asset-backed like credit card debt which is very common and quite expensive.
	Take special note of
	Student loans
	Mortgages
	Medical debts

	Personal loans
	Try to see if these debts can be separated, so you don't end up paying for something you don't own anymore. In most instances, this may not be possible, but it doesn't hurt to try.
Income tax returns for at least three years.	You can check the IRS website for more information if you're in the US.
Credit card statements, both joint and separate.	Deactivate all joint credit cards, ban any future charges, and open new ones in your name alone. This doesn't need to be done before the divorce as it might affect the judge's decisions. Ask your attorney and financial analyst for guidance before you make any move.
An inventory of property bought together (marital property) with receipts.	This will help determine the value of your contribution to the property when it was bought as well as appreciation

	or depreciation.
Insurance information.	If your spouse is a beneficiary of any of your insurance policies, remember that you have to change that. But, this doesn't need to be done before the divorce as it might affect the judge's decisions. Ask your attorney and financial analyst for guidance before you make any move.
Employee benefits and retirement information.	If your spouse is a beneficiary of any of your retirement or employment benefits as well, that has to be changed too. This doesn't need to be done before the divorce as it might affect the judge's decisions. Ask your attorney and financial analyst for guidance before you make any move.
Recent pay stubs.	As far back as three or six months should be adequate unless your attorney or the

	judge asks for more.
Nonmarital property inventory with receipts.	If there are properties owned before the marriage, get them appraised and ready.
Household inventory.	This is a list of the items in the house as well as their financial value.
Financial statements.	This shows the liabilities, assets, current income, and expenses for yourself, your spouse, and your children.
Household bills and receipts.	This shows your household expenses and is part of the financial statement. It's helpful to have it as a standalone document as well.
Bank account information both joint and separate.	Depending on your state laws, separating the finances for a divorced couple may be very complex. Closing or emptying joint and individual accounts may hurt your case in court. Instead, try to be as transparent as possible with your spending.

- If you're a low-income earner or not working, it's best to get sound financial information before negotiating for whatever asset you want. This is because different assets have different tax requirements. For example, most retirement assets are taxed on distributions, so you might have to pay tax if you end up with them, and the initial value of the money will be diminished. It may be better to opt for an asset like a money-market fund instead.

- Consider social security benefits. You may be eligible to get social security retirement or disability benefits from your ex based on their earning record. If you're within three months of age 62, and the marriage lasted for at least 10 years and you haven't remarried, then you can apply for ex-spousal benefits. You may not have to wait before they start collecting those benefits, but you can apply once the divorce is two years old. You can get more benefits if you wait till full retirement age before you apply. Even if you're receiving social security benefits already, you should still claim your ex-spousal benefits. You won't get the two of them combined, but you'll be paid the higher amount. Speak to your attorney or divorce finance analyst for better clarification. You just might opt to wait for ten years before divorce to access these benefits.

- Put a pause on big financial commitments. If you're planning something big like buying a new house or so, keep it on ice for now

This list is quite comprehensive but by no means exhaustive. You should definitely speak to your attorney and divorce financial analyst.

Financial Survival Checklist during the divorce

Admittedly, it's easy to get carried away by the divorce process, especially if it's long and drawn out. But it's important to stay focused on your finances even during this period.

Your key factors for consideration when it comes to financial decisions are your goals for your family and what you can actually afford. Don't forget that your once single household is now two separate households, which is as complex as it gets. It's completely normal to keep readjusting your budget as you go along. During the divorce, you should:

- Keep a record of how the money is spent. Your partner might be making some irresponsible financial decisions. You want to take note of that to bring up in court if needed later.

- Confirm your employment benefits with your employer. If you're working at an organization with an HR department, find out how divorce can impact your benefits.

- Consciously save money. This doesn't mean you should be too frugal but try to save as much as you can because unexpected costs are bound to come out of left field during a divorce.

- Set up your own checking accounts. If your attorney agrees, it may be time to get your account in your name. If you haven't already closed them, close these accounts and reopen new credit accounts, bank accounts, and even brokerage accounts if appropriate.

- Readjust your retirement accounts. Your divorce settlement, state laws, presence of a prenup, and the time of establishing your retirement accounts are important factors to consider when evaluating the impact of your divorce on your portfolio. It's essential to check out your portfolios and readjust them if necessary.

Financial Survival Checklist after the divorce

After the divorce is over, go over the settlement with your lawyer and analyst to understand its implications.

Evaluate your current financial status.

This checklist will provide some guidance:

- Change documents and accounts if necessary. If you're changing your last name, you should reflect that on your vital documents and accounts like your checking accounts, investment accounts, insurance policies, and creditors. Also, inform the DMV, your employer, and the Social Security Administration. Don't forget your will, estate plan, credit reports, insurance beneficiary accounts, property titles, and tax filing choices. Whew, that's a handful, but it's best to cover your bases.

- Stay observant. If you're dealing with a narc or a toxic partner, there's a high chance they might renege on a previous financial agreement. For example, they might promise to keep paying off your car loans even though they agree that you can keep the car. Sometimes they may not hold up their end of the bargain, and since the car title is in your name, the repossessed vehicle is considered debt cancellation by the IRS, and you have to claim that as income on your tax return. Keep tracking all financial obligations from your ex to stay safe. Discuss with your attorney or analyst for clarification.

Fix your credit

Now that you've done some basic cleanup, it's time to take an honest view of your finances. Your credit score has most likely been affected by this divorce, but that's to be expected. The first thing to do is to check your score from your credit bureau. I know it's not pretty but finding out your score can help you decide on a plan to build it back up. You may find this checklist helpful:

- Sort out all joint debts. While the court may have separated most of your financial responsibilities during the divorce, sometimes credit reports may not reflect all those changes. You may find out about joint accounts you were unaware of previously or notice that your ex has a mountain of debt on one of your cards. Getting a credit report will help you see what loans and cards are in your name as well as joint debt. If you realize that joint accounts are still open, write a letter to request account closure or name removal from your creditor. Then you can show each reporting agency the proof of credit closures. Doing this might affect your score even more, but by the time you establish your credit, your score will go back up.

- Create a plan to rebuild your credit. It doesn't have to be fancy; it could be an excel sheet with a timeline of all the actions needed with potential dates for them to be achieved. This should be highly customized to your unique financial situation. Speaking to a financial advisor may be required.

- Create a budget that accounts for your new income and expenses and alimony or child support, depending on whether you're paying or receiving them. All bills like groceries, utilities, repairs, insurance, and so on should be accounted for. This budget helps you determine your credit application and how much you can use without overspending.

- Establish your own lines of credit. This helps to rebuild your credit scores. Some credit cards are great for people who want to rebuild their score, like secured credit cards, which require a deposit before you can use them. This type of card helps you reestablish your credit-worthiness and lets you repay your bills.

- Pay your bills on time every month. This is very important and helps raise your score. Don't focus on your credit card bills alone; pay all your bills, like your student loans, medical bills, if any, and utilities, on time. If your ex-spouse still has to make some repayments for a debt in your name, it's important to make sure they stick to it.

- Stay consistent and be patient. Your credit score won't shoot up overnight, but every little action counts.

As always, speaking to your financial advisor might be necessary.

It's goal time

Setting goals is a great way to stay focused financially. Think about it, where do you want to be in two years, financially speaking? How much money do you want to have saved in five years? Have those foundation goals written somewhere, then break them down into bite-sized chunks. If you want to have 20k dollars saved in a year, what would your monthly budget look like?

This simple goal-setting guideline may be of help:

- Assess your situation now. Do you have an emergency fund? Are you funding your retirement accounts? Does your budget reflect your current situation and your goals?

- Consider ways to save as much money as possible. You can do this by packing lunch to work instead of buying lunch. Cancel your gym subscriptions and do home workouts or work out with friends. Re-examine your subscriptions and cancel the unnecessary ones. Embrace DIY and stop paying for things like washing your car, etc.

- Create a realistic budget. A good guideline is to use 50% of your income for essentials like food, housing, etc. Save 15% and use 35% to settle debts, plan vacations if necessary, and for entertainment for yourself and your kids. Your budget might change depending on your situation. Do you need to move out soon and pay a deposit on an apartment? Do you need to buy stuff like furniture and other essential household items? Consider that in your budget. But once your budget has been created, please stick to it.

- Set up an emergency fund. This is a non-negotiable goal, and it's best to have about three to six months of your expenses saved up in your emergency fund. Don't be discouraged, just start small. This should reflect in your budget.

- Once your debt is settled, you can work towards saving up for a small purchase like a trip or a night out, or even a new outfit. Then you can save for big purchases like a house or a car.

- Make sure your goals are Smart. This stands for Specific, Measurable, Attainable, Realistic, and Time-based goals.

- Specific goals help you make precise steps to achieving your goals. It's better to say you want to pay $300 to offset your credit card debt by the 20th of every month rather than writing, "I want to pay off my credit card debt every month."

- Measurable goals mean goals that can be quantified. So you're better off saying that you're putting away 150 dollars to fund a new business every month rather than saying you would like to save up for your business.

- Attainable goals are achievable goals. If you need, say, $5000 for a vacation in the next three months, you're not going to aim to save $2000 for the next couple of months on a $1500 monthly income and expenses of $1200. That's not attainable; instead, it creates unnecessary pressure. Set bite-sized goals that can be easily attained. This even helps to boost your morale as you find yourself achieving milestone after milestone.

- Realistic goals are like attainable goals. Consider your current financial situation before you set goals. If you had planned to save $300 this month but had an emergency payment due, it's more realistic to pay off that emergency bill.

- Timely goals give a timeline for you to achieve a goal. This helps to keep you on your toes and work to achieve it. Say you wanted to go on that $5000 vacation in two years; you can plan to save $210 every month.

Having a SMART mindset will help you see the value in every little milestone and help you achieve your goals.

Evaluate your budgeting skills and your spending habits. You might need to stop some things you used to do while married, like frequent trips. Instead, stay accountable to your financial goals and take the necessary steps to adjust your spending to your new life and goals. A financial planner would be invaluable at this phase.

- **Check your personal life**

Many people jump straight into the dating pool almost immediately after a divorce, but it's probably not the best thing for you to do right now. Focus on yourself, take time to heal, and take care of your kids. Learn how to survive as a newly single person. I know, I know, it sounds pretty dramatic, but it's true. You have to relearn a lot of stuff and focus on building yourself up. You could consciously start spending time with loved ones, take useful courses or classes, focus on being physically fit and eating healthy food or even work with a therapist.

The major areas to work on are:

- Your emotional well-being. You may not always be happy, and that's to be expected. Give yourself grace and focus on slowing down. You can improve this by practicing five minutes of meditation and self-reflection in the morning and at night. Journaling and focusing on positive things also help.

- Self-care. Write a physical and mental checklist to determine how effective your self-care habits might be. A physical checklist can include exercise, hair, skin, diet, outfits, etc. The mental checklist may have journaling, meditation, practicing gratitude, words of affirmation, or even spending more time outside. Pick one of these, start working on it, and move on to the next one. Remember, a little goes a long way.

- Your friendships and other relationships. You may have neglected one or two relationships during your divorce. Make a list of people you'd love to connect with and plan to reach out to each of them.

The key here is to be comfortable in your newly single skin. You have to take charge of this and focus on yourself. By the time you're ready for another partner, you'll begin to see the benefits of this.

Carry your kids along

It might be unintentional, but children are often neglected during a divorce. Or worse still, they may be treated as an afterthought. This makes for poor mental and emotional stability, which reflects behaviorally.

Divorcing a narcissistic ex is as much for the kids as it's for you, and you need to keep them at the forefront of your mind at every point. Divorce is quite traumatizing for kids, as we'll see in later chapters, so they need as much love, care, and attention as possible.

Let me pause here to say this: No, you're not a bad parent. You're trying your best, and your kids can see that. And guess what? They love you. It might not look like it or even feel like it, but they do. You just have to work on spending quality time with them as you attend to the demands of everyday life.

Is your ex moving to a new city, or are you? Who gets the children for what major holidays? Who gets them for long weekends? These are the issues to be discussed and clearly communicated.

Do you have a good support system? If yes, this is the perfect time to lean on them. Can you afford a babysitter? Can you afford therapy for your children? Can someone else, a parent or family member, step in for games and recitals if you're too busy? Answer these questions carefully while ensuring your children's safety and comfort are prioritized.

Sort out all legal issues

Here's the rub, dealing with a narc most certainly guarantees that there might be problems with childcare and other legal issues. It's possible to modify the divorce agreement as long as you both agree to the changes. Of course, this is best done on the advice of your lawyers.

Custody and visitation need to be examined and decided carefully. If you feel that your ex isn't keeping up their end of the bargain or supporting you with the kids, you can try to get a change of custody and visitation rights. Speak to your attorneys about it.

Contact your attorney immediately if there are issues with spousal support, like an inability to meet up with payments. They will advise you on the necessary actions to take.

Common issues that may crop up are:

- Settling new inheritances and wills. If an inheritance comes up after the divorce settlement, it will have to be assessed. You may need to refer back to your attorney and the court.

- Moving to a new state. Custody and visitation rights will have to be revisited by both parents if this happens.

- Remarriage can affect child visitation, and child support, among others.

Like I always say, a divorce is never the end but only the beginning. Taking things step by step, focusing on your healing, and prioritizing your children are super important at this stage.

Why am I finding it hard to move on?

"Do not look for healing at the feet of those who broke you,"-Rupi Kaur

I'll be the first to admit that divorces can be quite stressful. Feeling disconnected, sad or even lost after it is very natural. While you're focusing on the practical side of the divorce, getting your finances together, making sure the kids are settled, and so on, it's definitely easy to miss that pain you might feel.

You have to accept it. Even if you initiated the divorce, it's perfectly alright to feel this way. You could be feeling guilty about it, and trust me, a narcissist will exploit that sense of guilt as much as possible. If the divorce wasn't your idea, you could be unprepared for the change. It could be tough to accept the divorce, especially if you feel like you have no control over it. Sometimes you could just be feeling lonely, especially if your ex-partner took your social network with them. These things are very natural.

News flash, it doesn't go away. It doesn't disappear. You can't ignore it into oblivion. You gotta face it head-on. To do this, you have to examine the real reason behind it. What's stopping you from moving on? Here are a few possible reasons why you're finding it difficult to move on:

You're afraid

Yep, I'm coming right out with it. Fear is a very common reason to stay stuck. Fear of the unknown, fear of judgment, fear of humiliation, or even fear of failure. You name it. Anger is a common way of masking fear. If you're irrationally angry over minor issues, that could be a way to signal fear.

You can't imagine yourself back in the dating pool.

Dating these days can be very frightening. You hear stories of how people treat their prospective partners and dates and think, "Oh hell, no!" I feel you, and I hear that. Starting all over again with a new person could be the scariest thing ever. Swiping over profiles on tinder or whatever app is hottest right now can be very depressing. Your fear is valid, but it shouldn't hold you back. Why not focus on the positive?

You can't face the reality of divorce

Many people cope with trauma and hard times by dissociating themselves from the reality of things. You may find yourself romanticizing your previous marriage just to get through the divorce. If you catch yourself thinking stuff like your ex wasn't even that bad or exaggerating the happy moments and minimizing the sad ones in your marriage, you could be in these shoes. Escaping the present via delusions is tempting, but unfortunately, they do not last.

You can't forgive your spouse

The issue of forgiveness causes a lot of disagreement and annoyance whenever I bring it up. The prevailing sentiment is disbelief and anger. Why should you forgive your abuser? Half the time, they're not even sorry. You know they would do it again if they had the chance, so why would you be so silly as to forgive them? They don't even care for the kids. There's no way in hell you'll ever forgive them! Right?

Wrong. The truth here is that forgiveness is for your own benefit, not theirs. Never theirs. Holding on to your anger is like holding on to burning coal. The only person it hurts is you. Letting go might be hard, but it undoubtedly frees you up to pick peace, joy, and contentment. If you're in these shoes, consider forgiveness.

I've come to realize that the magnitude of fear is often greater than the object of fear. This means that your fear of anything is more than the actual value of fear attached to it. We often tend to overplay our fears such that we warp the reality of things. That's not ideal.

Figuring out why you're stuck is the first move to finding your way forward. I sincerely hope you'll take the time to find out exactly what's holding you back.

Is Divorce Grief Real?

"It's sad, something coming to an end. It cracks you open, in a way—cracks you open to feeling. When you try to avoid the pain, it creates greater pain," -Jennifer Aniston

Here's what I've found out, in the most amicable of divorces, there's a level of pain attached. Don't get me wrong, divorce is a highly personal process, and the odds are that leaving a narc is as messy and hurtful as it comes.

Considering the effects of the toxic relationship on your kids and probably the long, drawn-out battle that's a typical narcissistic inclined divorce, you're probably a ball of emotions.

Even if your narcissistic partner was the one to initiate the divorce, it's still a lot. The popular emotions you'd experience are anger definitely, despair, shame, regret, or maybe even jubilation at breaking free of an abusive partner.

One oft-overlooked emotion is grief. Most people simply do NOT want to accept that they could feel sad at the death of their marriage. I mean, they were constantly abusing you and the kids. They probably ruined your credit and bad-mouthed you to your friends. You're glad that you're no longer in those shoes, but somehow … you're sad that your marriage is over.

If you take some time to really reflect on your emotions, I would not be surprised to hear that you feel this way. The worst thing about divorce grief is that nobody might understand how you feel. Heck, you're even having a hard time accepting it; how much more are your family or loved ones just glad you're free?

As little as it seems, lack of validation of your feelings may compound it and make you feel lonelier or even depressed. Before you know it, you're carrying around the weight of your grief alone while trying to show up for your kids and everyone else every day.

Sure, losing a loved one is tragic, but losing a marriage isn't child's play. When you lose someone, you probably have a support system, people to share your grief and help you through it. This support is invaluable and helps a lot. In contrast, the lack of this type of support, commonly seen in divorces, can also be dangerous.

Unfortunately, there's no timeline for this grief; we can't say it'll go away after a week, a year, or five years. It's a process, and you'll most likely go through the stages of grief.

It's best to speak with someone you trust about this. Journaling also helps. I want you to know that your emotions are valid, and you'll get past this too. Trust me. Take as long as you need because by the time you come out on the other side, you'll be better off for it and your kids deserve that version of you.

Phases in divorce recovery

"Divorce shreds the muscles of our hearts so that they will hardly beat without a struggle."- E. Lockhart.

One statement I will always say over and over again, ad nauseam, is the fact that divorce is not an event. Divorce is not the ruling by the judge. It's not the feeling of freedom you might get. It's more than knowing you 'won', whatever that may mean to you.

Nope. It's a process. I'll say that again. It's not an event; it's a process. I daresay it's a traumatic process. In fact, if we're being precise, divorce has two parts: a legal phase and an emotional phase. Don't get me wrong; both parts can be daunting. But the emotional process might be, by far, the most traumatic. And like all traumatic processes, it needs careful healing at every step of the way.

I remember Sophie, a young newly-divorced mom of two, asking me this question, "*If you say that divorce is a process, how long does it take? When can I expect to stop feeling this way? When can I breathe again? I need to be whole for my kids.*"

I'll tell you the same thing I told her. Or if we're being technical here, I'll tell you what John McPhee said: "*It takes as long as it takes.*"

And rightly so. It's a journey, a highly personal one at that. It's one where you need to give yourself a lot of grace to get through. It's one where you need to shut out the world and its expectations or demands. You need to be selfish about this because this process demands your attention and commitment. You need to do the work. You need to prioritize yourself and take the time to work through it. You'll need strength, self-awareness, self-forgiveness, and a lot of self-love. But one thing is for sure; you'll get through this.

I'd like to say this loud and clear: divorce stages are not necessarily clear markers or an exact blueprint for how people process divorce. As true as that is, there is some value in categorizing the different emotions one might feel during this process. They help to give a sense of progression and a general idea of what to expect. These phases may start even before the legal proceedings, during or after. Different reactions apply to different people, and that's absolutely fine.

The Stages of Divorce

1. Denial

This is a classic response to traumatic situations. A sense of disbelief may lead to you trying to ignore the reality of the situation. This is a well-known coping technique and offers some sort of emotional protection at the beginning stages of divorce. This shock and denial may last as long as several months, a few weeks, or even a few days. Don't try to fight it, or else you might be overwhelmed. This is also very valid even if you initiated the process.

2. Emotional pain

This is the part where I caution against bad coping mechanisms like alcohol, recreational drugs, or reckless behavior. The fact remains that as the denial wears off, the pain of separation and a dawning realization that your marriage is dead will definitely set in. It may be accompanied by guilt and a lot of self-accusation. You may also feel a sense of remorse over your actions or lack thereof. Tears and isolation are common in this phase.

3. Anger

Your pain will soon give way to rage. You may find yourself lashing out at your partner, your children, or some other innocent party. This stage requires utmost attention because its effects could permanently damage your relationship with others like your children.

Releasing your emotions is entirely natural and should be encouraged; the trick is to do it safely. You may find yourself fixating on your ex, trying to contact them, or attacking them at any given chance. It's possible that they might be in that same phase and may meet you guns blazing.

You don't need a soothsayer to tell you this is potentially disastrous, especially for the kids. It's best to take some time away from your ex and spend it with a therapist or a loved one to help you work through it. If you're not careful, you may get stuck at this stage and keep experiencing the first three stages repeatedly.

4. Sad reflection

This might come like a wave of depression, despair, or isolation. It's common for your friends and loved ones to try to talk you out of it or cheer you up. While they mean well, it's important to experience this stage and accept your emotions. You may find yourself reminiscing over old memories and start to comprehend how much you're losing with the marriage. It's important to speak with a professional to help you work through it.

5. Adjustment and restructuring

It finally looks like you're getting used to your new life; you may experience a sense of calm and less tumultuous emotions, unlike before. Your sense of sadness, despair, and loneliness will reduce. You may recognize and look for practical solutions to the new problems you've identified. You may start to adapt to the idea of a life without your spouse. You need to look closely at your finances as well as any legal implications at this stage.

6. Acceptance and rebirth

One important point to note here is that acceptance is not equivalent to immediate happiness or contentment. You're simply accepting and dealing with the reality of your position. In time, you'll find that you can become happier, positive, and excited for the future. You'll start looking forward to the future, and you may even be able to think about the divorce and your spouse without bitterness or sadness. You'll start to find peace in the everyday motions of living. You'll start to connect better with your children and your loved ones.

It's important to note that your life may never look the same way it was. And you know what? That's OK too. You'll be happier, and you'll discover new sides of yourself that you were never aware of

This might sound like a myth or something far out of reach for you and your unique situation. But that's not true. It's entirely possible to get to this stage. You will get to this stage. I know it, and soon enough, you'll know it too.

Don't forget to be kind to yourself during this process.

How long does it take to heal from a divorce?

Even though we know that we can't put a number to emotional processes like divorce, it's still very normal to wonder how long it could take to get over it. Is there an average time to be expected? How soon can you feel like the old you again?

OK, so I have two things to point out here. The first is to say congratulations! Yes, I know it's shocking to hear that. But I say it because the fact that you're at this point where you'd like to 'get over' this is a very good sign of growth. It means that you've passed through the stages of divorce, or that you're almost done with the stages and are really willing to move on.

I'm not saying that you can't wonder when you'll be done at any stage, but the fact that you do wonder and truly mean it is important here. So, yay you! Also, if you're not here yet, that's fine as well. You'll get here too, and I'll be here to congratulate you. So yes, yay you!

The second thing I'd like to say, again for emphasis, is that you may never return to your old self. And that's fine. Like I say, give yourself grace, be open, and accepting. Better yet, love yourself in whatever form you are; that's what you deserve, no matter what.

Before we look at the magic number of years, months, or weeks it takes to move on, there are some factors to consider. Some may prolong your healing time, and some may hasten it up. They are:

Your kids

This might arguably be the most important factor to consider. If you have children with your ex, moving on may be more difficult than usual. Co-parenting will involve frequent interactions and constant communication. Admittedly, that may make moving on take longer.

Your personality type

If you're a naturally resilient person who can roll with the punches, you may find it easier to adapt to get over the divorce faster than someone who may not be able to handle change as well. If you're the type that doesn't accept change easily, you may find yourself taking longer to move on from your divorce.

Your time together

This includes the length of time you were together, even before you got married. If you were in a long relationship before marriage, it's likely that you may not move on as quickly as someone who dated their spouse for three months before they got married.

The nature of the relationship

We all know that it's easier to get over a relationship that was full of conflict and unhappiness in its majority. While you might feel some token of regret that it's over, you're more likely to move on fast. On the other hand, a relationship full of happy times and love will take longer to move on. If you were never fully committed to the relationship in the first place, you'd be able to get over it faster than someone with a deeper level of commitment to their relationship.

Presence of a support system

When it comes to moving on from divorce, it really does take a lot of support and care to recover. If you have ready access to your loved ones and even a therapist, you'll find that you will get over it faster than someone who doesn't have a good support system.

Your level of preparation for the divorce

In general, if you're the partner that initiated the divorce, or perhaps you suspected that a divorce was coming, you may have been subconsciously preparing yourself for it, and as such, you will find that it's easier to move on from it. If, however, you were unaware of the divorce, it may take longer to get over it, as the shock alone might take a while to dissipate.

After considering all these factors, is it possible to put a number to when you'll achieve total healing? Well, different studies have said different things. A finding published by Clarke-Stewart in 2006 estimated that it takes four years to get over a divorce. Another study says that it's complicated and can't be determined accurately (Lucas, 2005).

Another poll carried out by a dating website found that it takes 17 months and 26 days to get over a divorce (Reporter D. M 2010).

Here's my take on it, you can't really put a number to it. That can create unnecessary pressure and worry, which will worsen the whole situation. The best thing to do is focus on healing and love yourself. I know, it sounds cheesy, but it's true! OK, let's move on.

Steps to moving on after divorce

The process of moving on isn't easy. It could get even more frustrating when you're not getting practical advice on navigating this murky path from people.

While I love the fact that people mean well, when they try to encourage you or advise you to move on, most times they end up saying empty platitudes like 'Just try to move on' or 'you're much better off' or 'you'll feel better when you meet someone new' or the infamous 'just focus on the kids.'

Let's face it, sometimes, half the stress that comes with going through a divorce is parrying those types of comments, questions, and prompts. It's important to be able to firmly but politely shut them down when they come because they invariably do more harm than good.

Another important thing to watch out for is your self-esteem. Surviving a divorce can take a big hit on your self-esteem, and it can start a slow slide downhill before you even notice.

Here are a few practical steps to help you move on:

Ask for help.

I always start with this whenever I'm talking about coping with divorce. This is because discussing your feelings helps you process them better. Listening to yourself explaining your emotions can lead to you having lots of light bulb moments and making realizations that you probably didn't consider earlier. You can speak to a therapist or join a support group. Even if you're just talking to a friend who cares about you and can understand you, that's fine. Always ask for help, and always reach out whenever you need it.

Forgive yourself

Living through a divorce is incredibly hard; how much more surviving a toxic marriage and successfully leaving it? Doubly hard. It's easy to spiral into a cycle of self-blame and accusations leading to self-hatred and even self-neglect. Popular culture says a divorce means that you've failed your marriage. It's easy to internalize that message and let it run our thoughts.

However, examining yourself and vetting your thought process will help you see that it takes courage to leave and that you deserve love, respect, and affection like every other human being. Don't blame yourself for the marriage not working out; instead, try to take a holistic view of the marriage. More often than not, you'll find signs that show that it was never going to work anyway.

Keep the children out of the drama

I cannot overemphasize this. We can't argue the fact that divorce changes your kids. It affects their lives in so many ways, and the truth is, they didn't ask for it. Rather than trying to make your children hate your partner or bad-mouthing them to your kids, why not explain what is happening to them impartially? Trying to turn your children against your partner, no matter how toxic, always backfires.

Also, your children will better adjust to the divorce if they see that both parents are cooperative and demonstrate positive co-parenting. Develop an effective parenting plan with your ex and establish respectful communication as soon as possible. Ensure that you're making decisions that benefit the children first before anyone else. Sort out schedules for visitations, rules and punishments, bedtime and homework routines, chores and responsibilities, and means of communication. It may be best to agree on what you tell your children about the divorce.

Positive co-parenting helps your kids understand that even though you're not together as a couple anymore, you're still in agreement when it comes to them. That sense of stability helps them weather the effects of the divorce better.

Double down on your relationships

It's normal to lose some friends during a divorce. It's very tempting to withdraw from friends and family after a divorce. Resist the temptation to hibernate and make yourself stay in touch with your loved ones. This may mean going out when it's the last thing you feel like doing or being social when you just want to lie in bed. Keep at it. It's helpful because being around people you care about forces you to step out of your own head and allows you to experience the healing and happiness that comes with positive social interactions.

Remember to connect with only those that offer love, care, and positivity to you. It may be wise to avoid judgmental people or frenemies. If you need to, allow yourself to make new friends. You can do this by volunteering for something you're passionate about, learning a new hobby in a class or even inviting a friendly acquaintance for coffee or a walk. A great place to find like-minded people is in a support group for divorcees.

Get to know yourself better

If you take stock of yourself as a divorced person, you might be shocked to discover a lot of changes you previously did not notice. You may notice that your likes, wants, and dislikes have been greatly influenced by your ex-spouse. This is a good time to reclaim your interests and develop new ones. You may also benefit from spending more time outside, switching to a plant-based diet, or moving to a smaller place.

Make a deliberate effort to reconnect with yourself all over again. This is especially important if you're thinking of moving on to a new partner. You can't love anyone if you don't love yourself first.

Practice effective communication

Communicating with your ex may not be the most pleasant thing to do. Communicating with a narcissist may be likened to an exercise in futility. Still, you gotta do what you gotta do. So the best way to achieve this is to keep calm and be assertive. Sure, you feel angry or upset, but try not to let it show.

Instead, assert your boundaries. This can affect all aspects of your relationship with your narc ex. When it comes to communication, what're the best means of communication for you both? You may choose to limit it to emails, texts, or calls. You may choose to regulate the frequency of communications and lay down instances where communication is allowed. You may also want to limit the topics of conversation. For effectiveness, it's best to restrict it to matters concerning the children or other important issues like court dates or financial affairs. Try not to insult them or make sarcastic remarks. Keep all communications above board.

I'm not gonna pretend that it'll be easy. Far from it. But it is necessary. Practice reinforcing your boundaries before you speak with them. For example, if they shift the topic of conversation to something outside the agreed-upon limits, how will you handle it?

Saying something like "*That's not what's important right now*" or "*That's not what we agreed on; please let's get back to the topic at hand*" is a great way to reinforce your boundaries.

Allow yourself to mourn

Constructive reflection on the positive aspects of your marriage is allowed. It's tempting to ignore it and denounce the whole marriage, but it's actually quite healthy to acknowledge that you felt some happiness at some point during the marriage. It's okay to realize that you miss it. Accept those feelings and work through them.

However, the key word here is 'constructive'. This means you can only do this for so long and to a certain extent. Once you find that this is hampering you from moving on or even functioning, then it's time to stop and focus more on the positive. Sometimes, all it takes is a good, healthy cry or two.

Acknowledge your little wins

Being harsh on yourself seems to be part and parcel of experiencing a divorce. I'm here again to tell you that it's not so. Instead of focusing on your losses or disappointments, focus on the positives. Did you finally get that haircut you've been longing for secretly? That's a win! Did you lose five pounds last month? That calls for a celebration!

Celebrating every win, no matter how small, is a happiness booster. Achieving a goal, no matter how minute, feels really good if I do say so myself. Don't take my word for it; try it yourself!

I'm going in again with the fact that you need to focus on yourself first when it comes to healing. You need to be the best version of yourself for yourself and your kids. You deserve the time to grieve, heal, rediscover yourself, and love yourself.

Putting in the work is super important to your next growth phase. You need to be strong for the next thing we'll talk about. We need to look at the effects of narcissistic abuse on you. How can you tell if your relationship was toxic? How do you know if you're experiencing PTSD? How can you safeguard yourself from further manipulation and abuse from your narcissistic ex?

Come find out in the next chapter.

Chapter Two

The After-Effects Of Narcissistic Abuse

"A relationship with a narcissist in a nutshell: You will go from being the perfect love of their life to nothing you do is ever good enough. You will give everything and they will take it all and give you less and less in return. You will end up depleted, emotionally, mentally, spiritually, and probably financially, and then get blamed for it."
– Bree Bonchay

Have you heard that story about the frog that was placed in boiling water and immediately jumped out of the hot water? I don't blame him; the poor guy was not looking forward to being scalded within an inch of his life. If you have, keep reading, there's a plot twist.

When the frog was placed in a bowl of cold water, on the other hand, he relaxed and didn't try to escape. The water was placed on a heating source and started getting warmer slowly. The frog still didn't move. As the water kept getting warmer, the frog moved about a bit; he noticed something was off, but he still didn't jump out. Eventually, the water got so hot that the frog sat up and took notice.

Guess what he did next? He jumped out! Yep, he didn't wait till he got cooked before he jumped out; instead, he escaped successfully.

You're probably familiar with this story. At least you're familiar with the popular version of the story where the frog doesn't pay attention to the gentle but steady temperature change and eventually becomes cooked in the now-boiling water. You probably expected the story to end that way. Well, I'm sorry to disappoint you. Not.

I chose to rewrite the story. Now before you start protesting at that, I'd like to point out that you're doing the same thing too. You're rewriting your own story. You chose not to be a statistic for emotional abuse, and you chose to leave that toxic relationship. It was difficult, but you said goodbye to the narcissist. You won freedom and stability for yourself and your children.

You'll probably hear me say this à lot, but I'm proud of you. You did that. But now isn't the time to rest on the oars of your achievement. Because it's not over yet. You still have to interact with your ex. Your children might have no choice but to stay in close contact with them. And what about you? How has the toxic relationship affected you? Could it possibly be why you're not entirely happy, even though you're seemingly free?

Are you apprehensive about your next interaction with the narc? Or have you noticed that you're not the same person you were before your marriage? Don't panic.

The fact is being exposed to a narcissist for any period is bound to affect you. The key here is to first identify any effects of narcissistic abuse you may be experiencing. You might even be a victim of Post-Traumatic Stress Disorder (PTSD). You have to look for the signs and identify them.

The next step is to protect yourself from your toxic ex. Rest assured, some techniques can help, and we'll examine them all right here.

Was it truly a toxic relationship?

The first step to solving any problem is identifying the problem and admitting that it's there. It's a simple principle, but it's pretty effective. You may not be sure that your relationship was toxic. Heck, your ex might have convinced you that you were the problem or, even worse, told everyone else that you were the problem. No worries, we'll sort that out now.

Before we go any further, it's possible that you may feel silly or stupid as you go along this part and realize that your ex manipulated you in more ways than you were aware. Look, don't fret. Don't blame yourself. Remember that the problem is always them. That's who they are. It doesn't mean you're naive or dumb. Nope. It simply means that the problem lies with them.

So how can you tell if your marriage is toxic? Simple, it's toxic when there's an imbalance. It could be emotional, physical, or mental in nature. This will definitely lead to abuse and constant unhappiness for one or both parties. If you're regularly experiencing guilt, anger, shame, self-doubt, or depression because of your relationship, it's definitely toxic.

Now, let's get into the signs of toxicity in your marriage:

Constant fights and arguments

Don't get me wrong, conflict is a constant in most relationships, even healthy ones. In fact, it's a great way for a couple to learn more about themselves and grow together. So that means conflict is positive in a healthy partnership and leads to a positive outcome.

Not so for a toxic relationship. Did you notice that you had a lot of fights about the same issues over and over again? That was because the topics of contention were not clearly resolved, and your relationship didn't experience any growth in communication or deeper bond due to the conflict.

I'm glad you're outta there, but that was definitely a toxic relationship.

A feeling of exhaustion

If the thought of your spouse left you mentally drained or you were always tired and you could trace that exhaustion to your marriage, it was most likely a toxic one.

If your friends or loved ones noticed that you didn't seem to find joy in the usual things or they said that you had lost your spark, that's a very telling sign.

Let's be honest; you probably saw this coming from miles away in the relationship. You probably secretly denied it and tried your best to fight it off. But you know in your hearts of hearts that you were over it already. Do you recall that feeling that made you giddy with excitement at the mere thought of your partner? Your willingness to be around them as much as possible and the satisfaction they gave you?

Yeah. When you lost that and started feeling the exact opposite of those emotions, that's probably when the relationship transformed into a toxic mess.

Walking on eggshells around your partner

Were you constantly anxious about setting off your spouse? Were you afraid to offend or disappoint your partner? Did they yell at you or criticize you over trivial issues?

If you found yourself instinctively adjusting and readjusting yourself to be as passive as possible, or you were quick to say 'I'm sorry' even before you were accused, that's a red flag. It's doubly confirmed when you saw that you were trying to make everyone else around you as unobtrusive as possible. If you told your kids to 'stay quiet so they don't upset the other parent,' or you didn't want your family members over because they made your partner upset, or you tried to control the conversation at the dinner table to avoid topics that you knew would trigger them, you were definitely in a toxic relationship.

You were always trying to assure yourself and everyone that your relationship was great.

If you found yourself always talking about how awesome your partnership was to anyone who cared to listen or constantly having an internal debate over how great it was, that was your subconscious telling you that something was wrong.

Did you notice your friends never asked about your marriage, neither did they make the usual observations they would have made about the changes in your relationship, or you caught them rolling their eyes while you waxed poetic about your great love affair? Take a step back to reconsider.

I mean, if you were always on the defensive regarding your relationship and were always getting annoyed whenever anyone dared to ask too many questions or probe deeper, that was a red flag right there.

You couldn't bank on emotional support from your partner

You noticed that you instinctively stopped seeking emotional support from your spouse. In fact, you were more comfortable telling everyone else your emotional issues because you knew they'd pay better attention and even validate your feelings.

If you were always hurt because your partner often humiliated you in public or never considered your feelings before making moves, you're right! That relationship was as toxic as it could get.

Many a partner has wandered into the arms of someone else who appeared to fulfill all their needs. Honestly, emotional support is one of the main benefits of such an intimate relationship, and yes, its absence counts as toxicity. Glad you dodged that bullet.

Your spouse told a lot of lies.

If your partner told a lot of lies, that's already very fishy. Catching them in several lies meant there were probably other lies that you didn't know about. And what about when they tried to deny the lies and made you crazy for accusing them of lying?

Take a step back to examine those fibs and little white lies your partner was fond of telling. Did you notice that lying came easily to them? Did you ever find yourself marveling over how they could extricate themselves from awkward social situations because they could lie better than they could breathe?

I hate to drop this on you, but they were very toxic, and that relationship was already doomed. When you're done trying to defend yourself in your head (surely you were not so naive to get caught up with such a toxic person, right?), tell yourself that it's okay. The important thing is that you're out.

You stopped feeling like you were in control of your life.

Did you realize that you started making decisions that made your partner happy at your detriment? Or did you feel overwhelmed and suffocated because they made all the decisions for you? They enjoyed dictating every move you made, down to who you hung out with or what you wore. That may have seemed romantic initially, but it was a clear-cut sign of toxicity. You probably felt they were being possessive in a cute way at the time, but thankfully you can see that it definitely didn't turn out well.

You didn't communicate well with your spouse.

If your partner didn't pay attention whenever you tried to talk about your feelings or they seemed uninterested in hearing you out, that was a big sign of toxicity. If you never felt heard in your relationship and when you tried to bring up your concerns, they brushed them away and said you were overreacting or making it all up, that wasn't right then, and it sure as shooting isn't right now.

You might hate to face it, but that relationship was super toxic and unhealthy for you. Good riddance.

You were always in the wrong

Did you ever notice that your spouse was 'always right?' Were you frequently apologizing for all real and imagined wrongs? Or what about when you were sure they were wrong, but somehow you still apologized? That was a major red flag, especially if they blamed you all the time, and it seemed like you couldn't do anything right.

Your partner blackmailed you emotionally or threatened self-harm

Emotional manipulation is a sure sign of toxicity. If your partner tried to make you feel guilty or blamed you for all their shortcomings, it may have been a sign of open toxicity. More so when they threatened to harm themselves if you tried to leave or if you displeased them in some way.

That's a red flag, and even though you're out, they need to get help and proper treatment.

Identifying a toxic marriage is only the first step to a true resolution.

Taking stock of the manipulative signs of abuse you may have experienced is important because you need to protect yourself against them the next time you interact with your toxic ex.

Can You Experience PTSD From Being With a Narcissistic Partner

Post-Traumatic Stress Disorder (PTSD) is a condition caused by experiencing or witnessing a traumatic event. It could be a one-off event or a series of events, but it is characterized by being horrific or threatening to the victim in one way or another. Some examples of traumatic events include torture, slavery, domestic violence, child sexual abuse, or emotional abuse.

Being in an intimate relationship with a narcissist can damage your mental and emotional health and be considered a serious case of emotional and mental abuse. Sometimes, the narcissist might be violent and could abuse you physically. That also contributes to the trauma.

Now, this is where many people, and probably you, might get it twisted. Denying or minimizing narcissistic abuse is one of the worst responses to it. The fact remains that this type of abuse subjects the victim to much more than meets the eye. They have been subjected to constant emotional pain and backhanded forms of manipulation that are put in place to make them feel crazy. That's the mind-blowing part!

Imagine being abused by someone for so long and in so many different ways to leave the relationship still feeling like you're the problem? Yep. That's how a narc operates.

I'm not gonna blame anyone for feeling this way or falling for this. You know why? Because most people haven't even heard about narcissists in the first place. Or even if they have, they probably think a narc is someone who's vain, super self-absorbed, or arrogant. Maybe they have a pair of horns or a sign on their T-shirt that says 'toxic'. They never think it could be their own sweet, loving partner.

Remember that the standard operating procedure for a narcissist is to draw you in by showering you with an intense amount of love and attention from the get-go. You're probably remembering this phase right now when they seemed so perfect and attuned to you when you knew that you'd found the right person for you, the one that just always seemed to get you and was ready to go above and beyond just to show you how much they loved you. Until they stopped being that person and made it look like it was all your fault. Then you started scrambling to get them back to their old, romantic self, and then later resentment started setting in, and the long slide down this slippery slope continued. Guess what? That's exactly how they operate, and no, you're not dumb for falling for them, no matter what they might have made you think.

Human beings are pretty resilient, and I saw that firsthand when I spoke with Tyler, a man who was trying to recover from an eight-year stint in a toxic relationship with his wife.

"I had to leave the relationship because I was depressed and too much of a mess. I felt like a crazy person, and I didn't know what to do. I was fortunate to speak to a therapist who told me right off the bat that my ex was toxic. I didn't even know there was anything like Narcissistic Personality Disorder. I didn't even think there was anything wrong with her. I just assumed she became more difficult as a response to something I must have done, and I tried to handle it like a man. I knew I was majorly stressed in my marriage, but I kept pushing forward, taking it one day at a time, and just tried to keep existing through it all.

I decided to leave after eight years because I felt I was doing her a favor. The divorce was hellish for me because she kept fighting it and trying to prolong it. When I had a major heart attack a couple of months into the divorce, I realized that the effects of that toxic association could literally end me. I had to sit up and take my life into my own hands. I started working closely with my therapist, and I realized there were a lot of things I let slip, a lot of times I gave her another chance and rationalized her behavior. I was a pretty fit guy who was a gym rat, so it was hard to admit to anyone, let alone myself, that I'd been abused. But admitting that and making peace with it was the first step to true healing for me ... "

Ty's case is a classic misuse-of-adaptability situation. He kept adapting to each level of abuse without realizing or admitting just how tough it was for him. I bet that sounds really familiar to you right now. This happens more often than not and leaves most survivors broken, bitter, and more abused than they might have expected.

Just before we move on, I can hear someone wondering if Tyler was being a bit dramatic and if heart attacks can happen due to a toxic relationship. If this is you, then you're gonna want to read the next paragraphs very carefully to see just how emotional abuse and toxicity can affect you. Heck, you're gonna need to stay glued to the next few sections as well to get the complete story.

Like we said earlier, being in an intimate relationship with a narcissist is severe enough to cause PTSD. I'll do you one better and say that it doesn't stop there; most cases of narcissistic abuse are associated with Complex PTSD (CPTSD) (Plonka, 2019).

CPTSD is a disorder that is related to PTSD as the name suggests. But in this case, the traumatic event is repeated over a period of time instead of just one single event. Narcissistic abuse qualifies as one of those traumatic events that cause CPTSD.

PTSD is associated with symptoms like:

Relieving the traumatic event in the form of flashbacks or nightmares.

As a result of the abuse suffered, it is common to have nightmares about being stuck in the same situation or even lucid flashbacks that feel like you're right where you started. This may usually be accompanied by dizziness and nausea whenever the traumatic situation is recalled.

A change in belief about oneself and other people.

Being on the receiving end of so much abuse has a huge tendency to warp your mind and make you change what you believe about others as well as yourself. For example, if you were a trusting person who believed in other people's inherent goodness, you may suddenly believe that the world is an evil place with wicked people in it.

A state of hyperarousal.

This is a condition where you find yourself constantly alert or primed for a repeat of the traumatic situation. It's like you're constantly expecting a situation and bracing for a repeat. You may not find it easy to sleep well or concentrate. You may also find that you're startled by unexpected or loud noises.

On the other hand, in addition to these symptoms, complex PTSD may also cause:

An inability to regulate your emotions.

This means you're not safely able to control your feelings. For instance, you could be experiencing a depressive sadness and suddenly find yourself being uncontrollably angry at the same situation. This can be as a reaction to a seemingly minor event or an event similar to the original traumatic episode.

The bottom line is if your emotions are swinging wildly like an out-of-order pendulum, such that you can't even put a finger on your actual emotional state at any point, or you're stressed about the intensity of your emotions, you need to take a closer look at them.

A negative self-perception.

While the average person may not regard themselves very positively from time to time, someone with CPTSD has a very intense tendency to think the worst about themselves. Unfortunately, they blame themselves for the abuse they've gone through; icky emotions like shame and guilt come into the picture, and that manifests as self-neglect at best and intense self-hatred at worst. Unfortunately, this belief is so deeply ingrained that self-awareness and a lot of internal work is needed to recover from this. More on this later.

A switch in consciousness.

It's not uncommon to experience some form of dissociation when you have CTPSD. If you've observed that you sometimes feel detached or unconnected to your environment, your emotions, or even your body, this is a sure sign of complex PTSD. Some people may even experience periods of lost time where they couldn't recall what they did in that window of time. This could last for as little as five minutes or go on for days or weeks. All in all, this needs immediate attention from a licensed professional therapist, especially if you're losing chunks of time. A milder form of this could show up as a total loss of that specific traumatic memory or some parts of the traumatic event. This is obviously a coping mechanism and also needs attention.

A sprinkle of Stockholm syndrome or maybe not.

I'm pretty sure you've heard about Stockholm Syndrome. No? It's a sort of coping mechanism someone kidnapped may develop towards their kidnapper. So they start to have positive feelings towards their captors as time goes on. These feelings intensify as the period of captivity gets longer. Eventually, the captive may refuse to implicate their kidnapper or cooperate with the authorities to turn them in.

This may not happen in CPTSD, but you may either have positive feelings or misguided illusions about your narcissist partner and the abuse. You may find yourself giving total control of your life to your abuser or just going with the flow and being genuinely OK about it. Or so you think.

Another reaction could be an obsession with revenge or getting even with your abuser. None of these reactions are healthy, even though a need for revenge is understandable. They each need to be viewed under the lens of objectivity and self-healing not destructive revenge.

Another popular query I'd like to address here is that even if there's no physical abuse, the emotional component alone of narcissistic abuse is enough to cause CPTSD. But what exactly makes this trauma response so severe? A lot of work is still being done to find out how prolonged trauma affects us, but it has been shown that the stress response to trauma affects the hippocampus, the amygdala, and the prefrontal cortex of the brain such that these changes may be long-lasting. So as a response to this trauma, people with PTSD have a smaller hippocampus, a smaller Anterior Cingulate with decreased function, and an increased amygdala function (Bremner, 2006).

The body reacts to stress by producing cortisol, a hormone that triggers the 'flight or fight reflex' in the body. Cortisol has often been referred to as the 'stress hormone,' and rightly so. Again, people with PTSD have increased cortisol production as well as increased norepinephrine production, which intensifies the stress response (Bremner, 2006).

If you still think that narcissistic abuse is 'not a big deal,' especially if there was no physical violence, think again. I mean, science says it's kind of a big deal, so yeah. Look, all I'm concerned about is your healing, and the longer you minimize the effects of the abuse on you, the more you're putting off the healing process. This is incredibly important if you don't want to be stuck emotionally. I know I say this a lot, but that's how important it is. Even if you don't believe me, believe science!

While we're busting myths here, I want you also to know that the healing process isn't a piece of cake or a walk in the park, but by Jove, it's entirely worth it. The best thing about this process is that you can enjoy the benefits while still healing. I can't wait to walk you through it all!

Examining Narcissistic Victim Syndrome (NVS)

I know what you're thinking, and the answer is Yes.

Yes, there's a whole term for what victims of narcissistic abuse experience. That's how serious it is.

NVS describes the effects of toxic, narcissistic manipulation on a victim. It's not a mental health condition per se, but as we've seen in the previous sections, narcissistic abuse is serious.

We've agreed that PTSD is a possible and likely constant consequence of narcissistic exposure. But what else? What are the other effects? Can we see what narcissism looks like from the victim's angle? How do you even know if you're a victim of narcissistic abuse?

I personally don't like the term 'victim,' but as tempting as it is to want to scurry away from that description, I encourage you to accept it but only on the premise that you acknowledge that you're not stopping there. Yes, you may have been a victim, but that's not the end. You're moving on from the victim tag to the survivor tag. So, there's no way you're stopping in victim territory. No, sir, we do not do that here. Got it? Good.

So no. Don't internalize the shame you might feel in this section, and don't let the guilt or the resentment be your identity card. Nope. Keep it moving and swap it in for healing, growth, and self-acceptance. What you don't know is that when you make this swap, you get a huge self-love bonus card! It's a win-win situation for you and me. For you because you're winning and for me because I love to see you win more than anything.

So can we do this together? Can we examine your past with your toxic ex and see exactly how their actions affected you? Yes, we can!

You're probably familiar with this now, but narcissists operate in three stages. They entice and idealize their victims, and then they go ahead to devalue their victim before finally discarding them and moving on. I'd say it's like clockwork, but sometimes a narcissist may come back into your life after they're done with you, just like a toddler goes back to their abandoned toys once in a while.

If we were to examine a narcissist and maybe look deeper, at their very core, we'd find what I think of as a vortex or a swirling whirlpool of selfishness and entitlement. Or maybe we could liken it to a pool of quicksand that consumes anything unfortunate to tread on its surface and gulps them whole without a trace. This visual is a great way to understand their all-consuming need to control everyone and everything around them and manipulate events to portray them in the best possible light. That may not even sound harmful or dangerous until you realize that they do all these things at the expense of their victims. Everyone is expendable to them except when they're manipulating you for their own twisted satisfaction. It's like they're trying to stay warm, except that their victims are the sticks of wood they'll carelessly toss into the fire to get burnt up. Anything to keep them warm and cozy. Moreover, they'll poke through the ashes to check for wood chips that may still remain and turn them over to be burnt completely. Totally and completely.

I'm hitting you with these hard facts, not to make you hate them or see them as inhuman or some type of monster. I want you to realize the cold hard facts. This is how they are. This is what they are programmed to do. They might seem to mean well, or maybe they're not that bad but guess what? They'll always stay true to form. Especially if they're not getting any sort of professional help.

Narcissists are often idealized as being self-confident or self-assured, especially if they're the overt type. But this goes further than self-confidence into a warped superiority complex worsened by a lack of empathy. It's a whole lot to unpack, I know. But the psychology behind narcissism shows that their behavior and traits are there to cover the shame they feel fundamentally. That's right. So they do all these things to prove to themselves or reassure themselves that they have nothing to be ashamed of or hate about themselves. Except, they still have a big kernel of shame and self-doubt anyway. So the cycle continues. This information is very important for later, so hold on to it.

The truly sad part is that you've probably endured months and months of narcissistic abuse before you even realized you were abused. You've probably normalized this type of abuse to some extent, especially concerning finances. They're not above manipulating you financially to keep you right where they want you. As we look closely at NVS, you'll see how they did it, and then we'll see how we can bounce back from it.

I've found that it's helpful to identify the motivation behind the typical narc's behavior as well as the phases of their relationship with the victim. This closely correlates with the effects that most victims experience.

Here are a few signs of NVS:

You constantly felt like you were in the wrong.

This is very significant, and perhaps that could be why it's my first point. But once you realize there was a pervasive sense of apprehension in the relationship and that you were always looking for the best way to apologize to your ex 90% of the time, that's a huge component of NVS.

Narcissists will never take responsibility for any of the negative consequences of their actions. They would much rather make you the fall guy, convince you that you were the bad person in the whole situation, and make you apologize. When you do apologize, you can be sure they will milk that apology for more than what it's worth, make you feel as guilty as possible and yet still bring up that same issue at their earliest convenience. You might ask, how do they do all this? Why, by lying and manipulation.

That's how a typical narc responds to wrongdoing. If you look back on your relationship and you find that you were always apologizing to forestall anger or to prevent your narc ex from digging up your past mistakes to make you feel small, then that was abuse. You were a victim. How does that affect you moving forward? Great question.

Because their anger, sadness, or despair is always very convincing, you probably started believing that you could never do anything right. You probably started feeling helpless and maybe even thankful to them for choosing to stay with someone like you. I mean, who would want to be with someone who keeps making mistakes back-to-back? Like, how gracious could your ex be for taking you back after soooo many mistakes? An angel on Earth, right? Wrong.

I'm not a gambler, but I'm sure you still have that belief about yourself. That one that makes you so certain that you can't do anything right. And because the human mind starts to seek (and finds) confirmation for its beliefs, you may start to notice that other things in your life are going wrong and that you're to blame. See why NVS is a real thing?

You've realized that making decisions isn't the easiest for you.

Remember how we said that the second phase of narcissistic manipulation was the devaluation of their victim? Yeah, that comes into perfect play here.

So, you've probably realized that at some point after you got together with your ex, you started having arguments and disagreements. Mostly with them. They never liked anything you did and always had something negative to say about everything you said or did. They probably didn't come right out to say demeaning things about you. No, they usually used backhanded comments like, "*You really want to wear that dress? With your figure? Wow, hon, you're really bold.*" They may have even said something like that in public.

Something like, "*Let's make a toast to my wife for choosing to wear that dress against all odds. You're a brave woman, sweetie.*"

That definitely would have stung, but you probably couldn't protest without looking boorish, especially because they laughed and smacked your shoulder while giving the toast. That's just one instance. Now think back to all those little jabs they took at your hair, clothes, skin, the way you cooked, or anything else they might have used to take you down a notch or two.

Did you notice that you started asking for their opinion before making your decisions? Or maybe you just sat back and let them make all the decisions for you. I mean, that was less stressful than having to endure unnecessary criticism every day, right? No judgment here, I promise.

But now, can you see how you gradually stopped trusting your own decisions? How easy it was for you to make any change they asked, even after you'd made up your mind about something? Now that you're out, you may not be able to make those decisions easily again. You may find that you're constantly second-guessing yourself and losing confidence in making sound decisions. If you're being honest, you'll admit that your self-esteem took a big hit too.

I don't need to tell you that this period of your life requires you to make the best decisions for yourself and your kids. You need to stay confident and trust yourself. We'll see how to do that much later.

Other people couldn't see just how bad the abuse was for you.

One thing I always give the average narcissist credit for is their ability to play in the mud without getting their fancy clothes stained.

Don't know what I mean? Stay with me here.

The hallmark of narcissistic abuse and manipulation is subtlety. They can disguise their actions and deceive others such that they are perceived as innocent.

In fact, they are so good (or so bad) that you may not have picked up on what they were doing. You may recall times when you were left confused because you couldn't understand why your ex said or even did what they did. They often cleverly hide their tactics to make it seem like they are joking or making light of the issue. At the end of the day, when you try to tell your loved ones or close friends about the abuse, you probably heard them say stuff like *"maybe it was a mistake"* or *"they probably didn't mean it that way"* or *"surely, they would never do such a thing to you, they were so nice/gentle/soft-spoken ..."*

Now, this can be harmful in two ways. First, it makes you pull away from your loved ones because you can't get the needed support, understanding, and validation for your feelings about the abuse. This, in turn, makes you cut yourself off from that source of support.

Secondly, it can even make you wonder if you were truly abused or if it was all in your head. This is known as gaslighting, a popular tactic used by narcissists. It simply means that a narcissist can do or say something and then try to convince you that they didn't do or say that thing to make it look like it was all in your head. The overall aim of this action is to make you question your sanity and thought processes and eventually make you distrust yourself and instead rely on them more for guidance and direction about things happening around you.

If most of your family or loved ones couldn't see the abuse that you know you suffered, that is a typical narcissistic ploy, and you were victimized.

They've made you the fall guy.

Narcissists use smear campaigns to maintain their perfect images in public. They do this by attacking your image and making you look like the bad person in the story.

Now the average narc is very charming, and your ex most likely had a lot of your common friends and family members under their spell. So, almost everyone loved them and probably thought they hung the moon. If you noticed that a good portion of your shared friends and acquaintances didn't take your side after the divorce, then you probably were the subject of a nasty smear campaign.

Most narcs do this by twisting the facts and making you look bad behind your back or provoking you into responding angrily or harshly in public while seeming harmless themselves. This reinforces the idea that they are blameless while you're the monster.

Do this quick exercise and examine your various friendships in the wake of the divorce. Who left, and who stayed? What did they think about you? What did your ex say to them? You may try reaching out to them for clarification, but if this point resonated with you, you were a victim of narcissistic abuse.

Which of these signs did you experience? I want you to know that it's not necessary to have experienced these things to the highest severity. As long as you can identify with even some of these signs, you've been victimized.

Remember what we said. We're not staying in the victim zone, and in fact, we're moving on right about now.

Does Positive Psychology Help?

"Practicing positivity is like brushing our teeth—it doesn't last, so we have to repeat often. That's where the effort and practice come in."- Tina Hallis

Positive psychology has become the buzzword du jour for the self-help industry. Unfortunately, that means that it's been mistaken for what it's not by many people, and that's probably why many people discredit the concept of positive psychology.

So we'll take some time to see what positive psychology *isn't* before we look at what it actually is. It's not about being happy 24 hours a day or seven days a week. Nope, just because it's called positive doesn't mean that you'll need to focus on the brighter emotions to the exclusion of others. Instead, it tells us to acknowledge all emotions, even the negative ones.

It's not about thinking positive or self-help. I know many people make this association almost immediately when they hear the phrase 'positive psychology,' but it's not the same. Yes, both involve being optimistic, but only one is a science with appropriate research conducted and still ongoing. Take a wild guess as to which one I'm talking about.

Now that you're getting a pretty good idea of what positive psychology isn't, let's look at what it is. It's been defined in so many words and by a lot of people, but I'll go with Peterson's definition when he said that it's the scientific way to study human feelings, thoughts, and behaviors such that the focus is on the strengths instead of the weaknesses, improving on the good instead of repairing the bad in life and making 'average' lives great rather than only focusing on moving those who are struggling to 'normal'. In a nutshell, it's the study of what makes life worth living the most in a scientific manner (Peterson, 2008).

Another way to describe it would be to say that it's the study of the processes and conditions that help people live optimal lives (Gable, 2005). So yeah, positive psychology is all about finding out how people like you and I can live their best lives.

That means it looks at topics like gratitude, compassion, self-compassion, self-confidence, self-esteem, character strengths, happiness, life satisfaction, hope, elevation, and well-being. It also focuses on spreading this awareness to organizations and institutions to get them to apply these principles to their structure. Just imagine this – studies and experiments being carried out just so you could find the best way to live your best life. Sounds like a no-brainer! Sign me up, please!

The biggest benefit of positive psychology is also a mind-blowing principle and let me just take a moment to say that I was bowled over by how simple this principle is. Like it's something that's right in front of our noses and doesn't need any fancy equipment to apply. It's something you can start doing right now and see amazing results! I kid you not because as soon as I found out about it, I tested it out, and it truly blew me away.

Now just because I'm gushing about how simple it is doesn't mean it's easy. Nope. Sorry, got you there, didn't I? It's not easy. You have to put in the work. You have to be consistent and keep fighting to maintain your results. It sounds like a ton of work, but it's much easier than you imagine.

I know, I know, it looks like I'm contradicting myself, but I'm not.

I'm trying to say that this principle is very simple to understand and apply but requires consistency and dedication like every other thing worth having. That's it.

Are we on the same page? Great.

So this principle is *drum roll please* the power of shifting your perspective. Even a small change in how you view things can actually positively influence your quality of life and increase your sense of well-being. Adding just a little gratitude and optimism into your life will bring bigger benefits than you'd expect.

How does shifting your perspective work? Is it burying your head in the sand or insisting that the sky is blue even though it's glaringly obvious that it's a stormy gray? Nope. It's choosing to say, "*Sure, the sky is gray, and there are lots of clouds, and things aren't sunny right now. But these clouds have some silver linings, meaning something good is just around the corner. And even though it's about to rain, I'll see the rain as a force washing everything away and giving me a fresh start instead of thinking it's here to ruin everything I've worked for.*"

Positive psychology provides concrete findings and ways for you to improve your life. You've probably heard that money can't buy happiness. Well, having money can influence your happiness, but we tend to overestimate the impact of money on our happiness. So yeah, money isn't all that. It's important but doesn't contribute as much as you think it does to your happiness (Aknin, 2009). Then choosing to spend money on experiences makes you happier than buying stuff. I'm not saying you can't buy that Hermès Birkin you've had your eye on or that all-in-one lawn mower you want, but studies show that spending on experiences makes you happier (Howell, 2009). The same goes for spending money on other people. Have you noticed that you feel happier when you maybe buy a loved one a present, send them money, or even take them to lunch at their favorite restaurant? Now you know why! (Dune, 2008)

Another interesting fact is that positive psychology says it's okay to fake it till you make it! Yeah, intentionally choosing to feel happy, even though your current events dictate the opposite, will make you happier in the long run. This means you must actively cultivate a positive mood and put in the emotional work instead of half-heartedly pretending to be happy. This is where shifting your perspective comes in handy. Having a bad day? Think about something that makes you happy, focus on the positive feelings you'll get from that thought, and let that switch your mood to a positive one. Don't take my word for it; it's backed by science! (Scott, 2011).

I'm gonna be honest here and say that practicing positive psychology may look daunting, especially in the face of a divorce and the reality of co-parenting with a narcissist. I don't know about you, but I might be tempted to kick the person that tells me to 'be grateful' when it seems like my world is coming down around my ears and nothing seems to be going right for me – trust me, I don't believe in violence. Yes, gratitude might seem like the last thing you need to hear about, but the truth is it has its place.

Narcissistic abuse naturally leaves some sort of fear behind in you. What if the next person you meet is also a narcissist? What if you were victimized because you're all messed up inside, and the narc is drawn to that? What if your children are scarred for life because you got a divorce? The fears are never-ending and will drive you to make decisions that may do more harm than good in the long run. For example, choosing not to get involved with someone you're romantically interested in, even though your therapist says it's OK and you feel ready because you're scared to get burnt again isn't the greatest decision to make. What about refusing to examine yourself closely because you're scared you'll find out you're broken inside? So how can you manage these fears, let go of them and make better choices?

The answer is gratitude. A study among veterans who served in the Vietnam War found that those with lower PTSD rates practiced gratitude (Frederickson 2003). Another study was carried out among the 9-11 survivors, and it was found that gratitude lowered PTSD rates among them as well and improved their resilience (Kadashan,2006). Several other studies have shown that practicing gratitude positively impacts health, helps mitigate the effect of PTSD, and generally encourages recovery from traumatic experiences.

The best part is that practicing gratitude effectively shifts your perspective and will help you change how you see yourself. The end result is that instead of viewing a stressful situation as a threat to your well-being, you'll start to look at it as a challenge, one of many you'll overcome (Vernon, 2009). You'll learn to focus on things you can appreciate or value, and you'll start to see that you become more satisfied with life when you practice gratitude.

Two practical ways to start practicing gratitude right now are:

Start a gratitude journal

This is a great way to identify and meditate on the good things in your life. It helps to keep you in a positive state of mind. If you stick to writing in this journal for about two weeks, you'll see a difference in your sense of well-being, and you'll find that you're actually starting to feel grateful for more things. All you need is the notes app on your phone or a nice journal. I personally recommend a physical journal because it's less likely to distract you like your phone might. Also, I'm old-fashioned like that; sue me. This will take you a maximum of 15 minutes a day, even though it could be less. You can start with writing in it three times a week for a start and increasing your frequency as you get comfortable. The key here is to be intentional about it and to stay consistent.

Now I can almost see you rolling your eyes and thinking that you have little to be grateful for. I hear you. I know how that feels, and I have you covered too. Just go through the checklist and try it out.

Here's a little checklist to help you keep a gratitude journal (even when you don't have anything to be grateful for):

- Find a quiet, peaceful place to sit with your pen and journal.

- Think about the negative experience you've survived. Pick one thing you've gained since the divorce. It could be your free time, the fact that you no longer have to be around someone who demeans you, etc. Just pick one and write it down.

- Be as specific as possible. Instead of writing "*I'm grateful that I'm out of that abusive relationship*" why not write, "*I'm grateful that I can wear my hair however I want to wear it because being made to believe that I was ugly or that my beauty depended on how I wore my hair was weighing me down. I'm glad that I can now see it for the lie it was. Today, I'm wearing my hair down because my ex hates it when I do that, but I know I'm beautiful anyway. It's going to be a great day.*" See? Being specific is very important.

- Now think of the negative outcomes you've avoided or prevented. Don't take any positivity for granted. Write one down. For example, "*Even though I don't have primary custody of the kids as I wanted, I'm grateful that I still get to see them regularly, and I'm grateful for the free time I now have to work on myself and be a better person all round.*"

- Think about who you're grateful to. It could be your friends, parents, or even the judge. Pick one or two people and write why you're grateful for them. Remember to be as specific as possible. Go into as much detail as you want; there are no rules here.

- Think about what you still have. Sure you lost the house, but at least you could keep the dog. Or maybe you're left with a lot of debt, but at least you still have your job. Even if you can't point out anything that you have (which I doubt), be grateful that you're alive and on the right path to becoming your best self.

- Every time you approach these prompts, try to look at them from a fresh perspective and look at a different detail each time you write.

- Write about anything else you may be feeling grateful for. It could be the weather, a surprise visit from a friend, or a social media post that made you happy. Anything goes.

- Do this at a certain time, e.g., every morning as you take your morning coffee.

Voilà! There you have it. Will you try it?

Write a gratitude letter.

Keeping a journal is personal to you and should be private. However, identifying someone you're grateful for and telling them why is a great way to boost your sense of gratitude and well-being. It also improves your relationship with them. The very act of giving thanks also boosts your self-esteem, makes you more empathic, and can even help you sleep better. It basically takes you one step further.

Here's a simple checklist to get you started:

- Think about the person you're expressing gratitude to. What are you grateful for? Ensure there are no distractions and go as deep as you can. Are you grateful for their support? Do you appreciate the fact that they've always had your back? You can jot down all these points somewhere else, so you have all your ducks in a row.

- Now, write down what you've thought about. It doesn't have to be a conventional type of letter; there are no rules here. But try to be as specific as possible and leave no stone unturned.

- Write about how they made you feel and how their actions have affected you. Again be as specific as possible.

- Add a compliment for good measure.

Of course, you can write it as an email if you prefer that to physical letters. Remember that the letter doesn't have to be fancy or poetic; you don't have to use fancy stationery or a quill pen. Just remember that you're trying to communicate with someone and express gratitude. That's it.

The bottom line here is that practicing gratitude and by extension, positive psychology will give you a turbo boost on your road to healing.

A fair note of warning here, practicing positive psychology should not lead you to do things like getting back with your toxic ex or believing that you owe them another chance or anything like that. No sir. Instead, it encourages you to acknowledge your feelings and embrace reality while focusing on the positive aspects. It will never require you to put your life in danger or encourage a loss of self-respect or disrespect from anyone. That's why this book is here to guide you.

Safeguarding yourself after divorcing a narcissist

"When a toxic person can no longer control you, they will try to control how others see you. The misinformation will feel unfair, but you stay above it, trusting that other people will eventually see the truth just like you did." — Jill Blakeway

Everyone makes mistakes. That's normal. In fact, we learn that the next best thing to do after making a mistake is fix it. Good thinking, right? One big mistake I see people who were once involved with narcissists make is to assume that leaving them or divorcing them is the end of the road. My friend, that's a big mistake to make, and I hope you're not making it.

If you're in those shoes, you're in the right place! We're going to fix it. We're going to see how to stay safe and protected from narcissistic tactics.

A typical narc is comfortable with lying and getting others to believe alternate versions of reality to suit their own purposes. At the core of it all, they are intoxicated by fantasies of their success, power, and self-importance. In an ideal world, we would all exist to serve a narc, but since the world isn't ideal, they will carve out a little kingdom for themselves where they get to manipulate and control everyone as much as possible. Asking for a divorce means trying to snatch their kingdom away from them and making them look bad.

Two things they detest.

So they fight. They make the divorce process as long and as drawn out as possible. They ignore court orders, lose documents, undermine your efforts, lie about you in court and try to paint you as the bad guy. They know they're making things very difficult for you and don't care because they want to make you pay. They won't stop until they feel like they've gotten their just deserts. Guess what? They'll never stop even then. They might pause, especially if they have another victim in their sights, but they'll come right back after a while. You can take that to the bank.

I wasn't too shocked when I heard about Joshua's ordeal after he divorced his narcissist wife. He was so relieved that they were over the divorce and ready to move on with his life and the kids. But she wasn't. She kept lying to the kids about him, showing up unannounced at his job, and stalking him while he was on dates. He became very frustrated when he discovered that she would contact the women he was interested in and lie to them about him. He was frustrated, and he didn't know what to do. I'll tell you what I told him. The real battle comes after the divorce. Not before or during.

Here's how to stay sane and protect yourself from your narcissist ex:

Cut them off.

This is the first thing that should be done. Obviously as your co-parent, you can't entirely cut off communication with your ex, but you can limit it. It may seem extreme, especially to your mutual friends, but remember that most people don't know your ex as well as you do. You can be sure that your ex can be as smooth and charming as they need to be to get people on their side.

Cutting them off means modifying your communication with them. This may look like it may not be possible, especially when they start pulling their tactics. But it is, and it's necessary. When you cut them off, you essentially control their access to you and reduce your exposure to their hurtful words and behaviors for the most part. You're also putting yourself well out of their reach because they enjoy watching you react to their antics.

Limiting communication with them is the first step to setting clear boundaries, so it should be firmly adhered to. Make sure that your conversations are only about your children. Any other topic should not be entertained. Instead of talking or texting over the phone, choose emails as the preferred communication medium. This will help keep them in line and prevent any escalations. Well, even if they are nasty or insulting to you, it's all documented, so it can be used as proof if needed. Using clear subject lines is very important and keep your emails succinct and on-topic. Don't be nasty, sarcastic, or rude, no matter how much you want to. Let your emails be neutral, informative, and firm. A good example is this:

Subject line: Annabelle's Dance Rehearsal.

Hello,

I'm aware that I'm taking Annabelle this weekend, and I'll pick her up after rehearsal. Please ensure that she's all packed and set to go for the weekend.

Thanks.

Dan.

See? Simple, short and sweet.

Of course, your ex will try to push your boundaries by calling without any notice or sending you texts about issues you've already agreed not to discuss. Do not engage. I recommend blocking them and limiting them from accessing your social media. Maintain this limited contact physically too. Plan your schedule such that you never have to see them, or even if you do, it has to be very brief, with no communication whatsoever.

- Take care of yourself

This might arguably be the most important point here. Taking care of yourself, loving yourself, healing yourself is the best revenge and protection from a narcissist. The pattern of abuse you've faced has left its mark on you, and you need to realize that. Yes, you have to co-parent with them, but you're not married to them anymore. Focus on your own healing. Take your self-care seriously, start seeing a therapist, value your friendships and spend time with the people who make you feel loved and wanted.

Practice self-love and self-compassion, reassure yourself that there's nothing wrong with you. You know those cheap shots your ex used to take? Those ones where they talk about body or the fact that you don't have much money or maybe it's the fact that you cheated on them once. Think about it. What's that one thing they could say or do that gets a rise out of you? Or makes you wince or even grimace? What are those areas that you could call your weak spots? Identify them and work on accepting them. The goal here is to shore up your defenses such that you won't fall for their old tricks.

- **Face the facts**

Guess what? Your narc ex won't ever change. They'll never consider the children or play nice for their sake. They'll never decide to do things the easy way for you. They'll definitely not take it easy on you. Do you copy? THEY WILL NEVER CHANGE.

That's on them, not you. Understand this and accept it. You need to view the situation realistically to stay on top of it.

- **Protect your relationship with your kids**

Unfortunately, your kids will have to spend time with your ex. This means that for a particular amount of time, they will be exposed to your ex and their tactics. Stuff like bad-mouthing you, lying to them about you, neglecting them, or deliberately ignoring the agreed-upon rules to annoy you isn't off the table.

In this scenario, the best thing to do is to work on maintaining a genuine relationship with your kids. Encourage them to come to you if they have any questions or doubts. When they do, try your best to answer them as neutrally as possible. No ranting about your ex, no name-calling or complaining.

Just stick to the facts as they are. Remember also that your kids may get caught up in the middle of the separation and react in different ways. This is the perfect time to apply empathy, consider their feelings, and connect deeply with them. Help them work through their feelings at every stage. You may be the only parent providing this kind of emotional support, so it's important that you do this.

- **Put everything into writing**

Drawing up a legally backed plan for parenting may seem excessive at first but will come in handy. A legal parenting plan is the first step and the backbone to getting everything documented. This serves as a custody agreement and can include things like visitation rights and schedules, holiday plans, payment for bills not covered by child support down to the percentage, and other things like that.

It's drawn up by your lawyer, agreed upon by both parties, and is tenable in court. It's a great instrument because a third party has to enforce the terms outlined in the plan. Make sure your plan is as detailed as possible. Do you want to be notified before your ex takes your kids out of state while they're visiting? Make sure it's in there. Is there a joint college fund account for your kids? How much should each party contribute? Put it in there.

Another important thing to document is every offense your ex commits. For example, if they missed a pickup or came late to a drop off, document it. You could send an email to them stating what they did, so that could serve as proof. Did they miss a payment? Print out your account statement and keep it as proof. Basically, have as much evidence as possible. It's okay to bring in a third, unbiased party as a witness. These things can come in handy later if you're trying to get sole custody. Everything matters, so write them down.

If you've noticed that they've breached the agreement, you may have to act fast in some cases. For example, if they miss a child support payment, you can file a contempt action in the court immediately. This communicates that you're serious about your terms and may dissuade them from repeating them.

Keep your boundaries firm

You've already started this by limiting communication, so take it a step further by defining your relationship with them. Ideally, you shouldn't have much contact with them, nor should you entertain random meetings or discussions about your marriage.

Remember how loving your ex was when you first got together with them? Well, they're not above reverting to their loving, attentive self to try to get you to lower those boundaries. This person has spent a significant amount of time with you and is sure to know your weak points. Don't underestimate them. Limit physical meetings. If they must happen, limit the scope of engagement. For example, refuse to discuss the divorce or your marriage; instead, keep the conversation centered around your kids.

I know transitioning from someone who's had their boundaries violated or who probably didn't have healthy boundaries before to someone who's setting firm boundaries is not easy, so here are some tips to help you cope:

- Take back control of your life. You may realize that you've fallen into the habit of doing things or thinking in a particular way because that's how your ex saw you. Take back your control by being responsible for your choices. Do you hate being spoken to disrespectfully? Decide that if your ex ever comes off as disrespectful, you'll end the conversation immediately.

- Make your home your safe space. Do not allow your ex to come into your home or feel comfortable walking into your house. Ensure they do not have any belongings or any reasons to come in. Decide that pick-ups and drop-offs should be done outside the house. Don't hesitate to close the door in their face if they try to cross this boundary.

- Never admit to making a mistake or apologize to them. That's like giving them ammunition to hurt you and could take you right back to your mental state while you were being abused. Instead, keep your communications short and be firm about it. We mean business over here.

- Take a break. This seems weird, right? But the truth is putting up boundaries, maintaining them, and obsessing over them can be very draining. Decide that you'll stop thinking about your ex or the divorce and instead focus on non-divorce-related stuff from a particular time every day. You could use that time to bond with your kids, read a book or do something fun for yourself.

- Keep making it up as you go. Boundaries are not made to be set in stone, and you can keep tweaking them till you find what works. For example, if drop-offs at the porch always end up in screaming matches and you can't control yourself, why not choose a public place like the park close to the house? Most narcissists want to be perceived as good by everyone, so they are more likely to stay composed in the future. Feel free to keep resetting your boundaries. You don't have to explain anything to your ex; simply inform them of the changes if it concerns them.

Well? Following this checklist should see you well on your way to setting and maintaining your boundaries. The fun part is that you expand this list as you go along.

Notice how I didn't emphasize friends and family? That's deliberate. Sometimes your ex may have isolated you from your support system or turned them against you, but that doesn't mean you can't protect yourself without their support. I want you to understand that you're capable of doing anything you set your mind to. If you have a supportive network, great, but if you don't have one? Guess what? You'll still get stuff done and take charge of your life. Because again, you can do anything you set your mind to, and if you've come this far, heck, then there's no stopping you.

Oops, guess I just practiced a bit of positive psychology back there. Hey don't blame me, it works. In the next chapter, we'll see how you can make better financial sense of your life after this divorce. We'll also look at what you need to do when you *don't* have a supportive network of family and friends. I told you I had something for everyone in this book, didn't I? See you there!

Chapter Three

Clearing The Mess After

"Stop trying to get validation from people who can't or won't acknowledge your feelings. This reflects their inability to empathize. It's a failure on their part and has nothing to do with you."
— Jacqueline Simon Gunn

Jane was practically in pieces. She was a mess. We met through a mutual friend and soon got to discuss her divorce with her ex. It started small; I noticed her voice was getting softer, and her eyes had a suspiciously glassy sheen. Before I could say 'jack,' she burst out in loud sobs and bawled her eyes out.

I was shocked, but I comforted her as best as I could and asked why she was so upset. She said:

"It's such a huge relief to talk with someone who's so accepting and supportive about my divorce. My family and friends think I'm a jealous, impatient child for divorcing my ex.

I met Randy when I was 22 and very naive. He seemed like all I'd ever wanted in a man; he came complete with the qualities I didn't even know I needed in a man. We were so perfect for each other and quickly fell in love.

Because I'd had a sheltered upbringing, my parents were very much against my marrying him just six months after we met. Randy met with them to try to convince them that I was in safe hands, but my dad was especially stubborn and insisted that

I wait at least a year extra before marrying him and that he had to join our church, where my father was the lead pastor. I thought he was just being difficult so I declared that I would marry Randy come hell or highwater.

After a lot of pressure from my mom and other family members, my dad finally caved and agreed to see us wed as planned. I was so happy! After two months, I got married, and we were happy together.

Until we stopped being happy. I started noticing that he would ignore me for days on end and didn't seem to love spending time with me anymore. By this time, I had stopped going for Sunday dinners with my parents because he wasn't comfortable with them, and I stopped hanging out with my friends because he said they didn't support our marriage, just like my dad. Whenever I went to see my parents, I tried to explain to my mom that Randy was changing. But she said I'd made my bed and had to lie in it.

Fast forward to three years later, and my relationship with Randy had devolved into a horrible caricature of what it once was. We were constantly arguing, and I discovered he was cheating on me with some ladies from my church. Go figure. I didn't realize it, but he was spending time at my parents' house and feeding them lies about our marriage. He manipulated my dad's fear of seeing me married so early and young. He told my dad that I had opted to stop going to church, and I now had divorced women as friends. He told them that I said I didn't want to work anymore, even though he was the one that insisted that I stop work so that I could focus on our kids. Oh, we have two kids, a four-year-old and a two-year-old.

I've never seen a father as apathetic as Randy. He would ignore the kids and yell at them for fussing too much. He only enjoyed handling them when we were out or with my parents. My dad tried to approach me twice to talk about my marriage, but he just ended up telling me to face my relationship and my walk with God squarely. Things went from bad to worse, and I decided I wanted a divorce and was taking the kids.

When I told my mum, she told me not to do that and said I had to endure my marriage for love's sake. She reminded me how much I had fought for Randy when we first met and said that divorce wasn't an option. I told my dad about the divorce and got the same answer. He said I was being flighty and spoiled and had to sit down and work on being the best mother to my kids and wife to my husband. I spent a lot of time crying because no one was ready to support me. My parents thought I needed to stay in the marriage, and the few friends I had, hinted that they wouldn't want to be associated with a divorced woman. They said that whatever was wrong with the marriage would be fine; Randy didn't hit me, and he seemed nice and respectable.

I called the divorce off twice because of this, but I found a therapist who held my hands through it and encouraged me. After the divorce, I was shocked because my family kept setting me up to see Randy without my consent. My mom believed we needed to get back together, but my dad refused to speak to me because I had shamed him. My ex kept up the innocent, wronged husband facade and kept setting me up to have an emotional showdown whenever we were around my parents. Eventually, I had to stop visiting them and moved away to another city with the kids for my sanity. But I miss them so much. I miss my mom. I miss my dad and the gentle way he'd call me 'baby girl' while hugging me. Is my family gone forever? Have I lost them? How do I make them see what I'm really going through? I've never been so distant from my parents, and I really don't know what to do anymore …"

Poor Jane. Unfortunately, her story is more common than you might expect. Sometimes, your family and friends may not be on your side when you have to battle a narc. Sometimes they may have fallen for your ex's charms and taken their side. They may even believe utter lies about you, but you don't know where and how to start. How do you cope? How do you get the support you need? Keep reading.

What to do When Your Friends and Family Are Not Being Supportive

The fact remains that going through a divorce is hard. Divorcing a toxic spouse is ten times harder if I'm being very euphemistic. Having to do all that without a support system? It could be hellish. Heck, let's not play around here; it will be hellish.

If you have friends that are couples, you may notice that some of them do not come around like they used to before. Some of them may have chosen sides, and they may have gone with your ex. Or they might even choose to avoid both of you entirely because they might be scared that the divorce could be contagious.

Your relationship with your parents is the one you've been involved in the longest. Same goes for the rest of your family. I'm not denying that these relationships could be dysfunctional, but they are certainly important. This is why having their support through such a difficult time would be ideal. Unfortunately, it's not always like that, and your parents could oppose your divorce for several reasons. They may not even be capable of offering the support you need. But before you conclude that you don't need their support anyway and try to do it all by yourself, let's examine the possible reasons why they may not want you to go through with that divorce and how you can address it.

Your parents will never stop seeing you as their kid, and it's not far-fetched to imagine that they might never stop treating you like a child, no matter how old you are or how many children you have. I'm sure you can relate to that feeling that seems to come hand-in-hand with parenthood. But if they are treating you like a child and not respecting your rights to make the best decision for yourself, it may seem hurtful or like they don't care about you. Don't throw the baby out with the bathwater yet. Remember that they may not understand the full scope of abuse your ex has subjected you to. Like any self-respecting narc out there, your ex is sure to have been as pleasant and nice as possible to your parents. They may have gone ahead to subtly imply that the problems lie with you. They could also have analyzed your parents' fears and used that to manipulate them and lie to them. Often, you may have been too busy trying to handle the abuse yourself to see what they were doing then. Their tactics may not be enough to turn your parents against you, but they could be sufficient to make them doubt you or underestimate whatever you may have to say about your toxic ex. This does not necessarily mean they are bad people; they are just victims too.

Your parents were certainly raised with a different orientation than you. They may be part of the school of thought that says that marriage is for life and you should look towards repairing it before you fix it. Naturally, they want to enforce their beliefs on you, or they might try to punish you for not doing what they say by withdrawing their support or leaving you to face the music alone.

They may not like the stigma of having their kid divorced, especially if their culture frowns against it. Their own marriage may not even be happy, but they chose to stick with it probably because of their cultural beliefs and their children, and they expect you to do the same.

They could be scared of the effects of a divorce on their grandchildren. They may not want them to grow up in a broken home or experience the negative side effects of that kind of situation. If your parents are divorced, they could be scared that you're making the same mistake that they made and may feel like they've failed at parenting you.

You need to sit with them to try to understand what their reasons are. Try to communicate that you feel like you need to do what's best for you. Help them understand that sometimes divorce might be healthier in the long run for your kids.

Don't be afraid to ask them for the type of support you need. If you need them to watch the kids or just provide a safe space where you can unburden yourself, tell them. Remind them that you also deserve to be happy, and they need to let you find your own happiness.

The same goes for the rest of your family and friends. If you truly value the relationship, try to see where they're at. If you feel like you can change their mind, give it a try. Ultimately, you need to remember that your peace of mind is paramount, and you might need to let go of these relationships if they no longer serve you.

If you truly can't find any form of support from your loved ones, don't panic. Search for support groups online or nearby. You would be surprised to see that many people may be able to relate to exactly what you're going through, which matters a lot. You can also form new friendships and be more social. But don't feel pressured to burden your tentative relationships with your divorce, especially if you are uncomfortable talking about it.

It might be difficult, but I know you can do it.

Handling the Gossip and Disapproving looks

You may not be prepared for so many aspects of a divorce. You may have steeled yourself to be a single parent. You may have sat your kids down and tried explaining what was happening to them.

You may even have signed up for therapy to help you handle it. I'm sure you researched and discovered that divorcing a narc would be tough. Maybe you could say that you're prepared for that. Maybe you could even say you're over the marriage and glad to be done with the abuse.

What about you, though? What about the gossip? What about the stares? Can your mental health handle it? Oh, and you can bet that your ex has gone ahead of you to run a very potent smear campaign against you. I'm not a gambler, but I could definitely put money on it, and to be honest, you should too.

There are so many ways this could hurt you, so many circles that have people who are interested in your life. I remember watching an episode of a show where a man was heard sobbing loudly in his office all day. All his co-workers were scared to ask what was wrong with him. And then, by the middle of the day, word started spreading that he had cancer and had just been diagnosed with six months to live. Where did it start from? Your guess is as good as mine. Everyone was devastated as you can imagine, and they all gathered in front of his cubicle at the end of the day to see what they could do. One brave soul decided to walk in to ask what was wrong. The weeping man sadly told his co-worker that his wife had asked for a divorce. To his surprise, his co-worker said, "Oh, thank God!" and ran outside to tell everyone that "He's only getting a divorce!" At that statement, a loud cheer rose up in the office, and everyone came in to congratulate the crying man on his divorce. I can only imagine how gobsmacked the soon-to-be divorced guy must have felt!

Anyhow, news of your divorce might sometimes not meet loud cheers and felicitations in your office. You could be met with whispers, stares, outright laughter, and even discrimination by others. Some predatory co-workers might seize the chance to take on your projects while claiming that you're not mentally fit to attend to them. It could be a whole lot, lemme tell you.

How about social media? Have you thought about that? Do you have to change your Facebook status from married to single? I'm not gonna lie; it might be humiliating to have to do that. But thankfully, there is a great way to handle gossip and keep your dignity. You'll need a bit of a stiff upper lip, but it's definitely doable.

Here's a short guide to handling these situations:

Protect your kids and your family members

We all know that celebrity divorces can be messy. I mean if you pick up your favorite tabloid or switch on the TV, you might find some divorce being dragged and devoured by the press. Maybe your divorce isn't that huge, but on some level, the same thing will happen to you.

Your first concern should be your kids and immediate family members. Gossip on social media, at work, or even at school concerning your kids should be handled immediately and shut down decisively. You may need to visit your child's teacher and explain what's happening. You could ask them for their thoughts or if they could support your child through this difficult time. You should also ask them to tell you about any incidents they may notice concerning your child. If your ex is a high-profile person, they may have extended the smear campaign to affect your kids. If the gossip is telling negatively on your children, that is, if you notice they are getting into fights or unusually dull and moody, you may need to consider withdrawing them from school entirely.

It may seem drastic, but the aftereffects of these situations can impact your kids significantly even when they get older, so you want to be as proactive as possible and remove them from situations where this kind of gossip is rampant. If a family member always talks about the divorce in front of your children, ask them to stop. If they can't, you may need to stop them from coming around your children. Set clear boundaries about this with your family and encourage your children to avoid situations where there may be talks about the split.

If it's a high-profile case, you may need to control their social media use and place privacy settings on their computers. The point is to insulate them from all the hateful speculation and gossip for as long as possible.

Don't engage on social media

Trolls. They are everywhere. Under the nearest bridge, in the darkest caves, and right there in your phone. You can trust that there may be comments or posts designed to hurt you on social media. Do not respond. Do not engage. Your ex may resort to creating fake accounts to stalk and troll you. Simply delete their comments, block them, and restrict them as much as possible.

Well-meaning people or members of your community may say hateful things on social media. Again do not respond openly. If you have a personal connection with the poster, you may reach out to them to correct their assumptions and ask them to desist from talking about your divorce online. If you don't have a personal number or a means of connection to that person outside of social media, their opinions probably shouldn't sway you. Just delete their comments, block them if needed, and keep it moving.

Now, let's talk about you. You need to watch yourself online. It may be very tempting to make personal posts that may subtly insult your ex or openly shame them. It's even more tempting when they've done the same to you on their social media. But remember, when they go low, we go higher. That means that you should not engage them. Even if it's just to correct a lie or silence à misconception, don't do it. Just don't. If your life or source of income is dependent on your personal brand, you may make a short, brief statement for the record. But nothing personal or degrading. No details about your toxic ex or their behaviors.

If you feel the need to share, write in a journal or vent to a trusted person. Social media is the last place to exchange potshots at each other.

Squash the rumors face to face

Maybe you're in a corner of the office kitchen and hear two people talking about your divorce. Or you overhear some false whispers about it in the hallway. This scenario is very possible, especially if your ex works in the same building or office as you do.

Instead of slinking away in defeat, call out the gossips and denounce their lies. Also, tell them that you don't condone being spoken about negatively. Do it as respectfully and professionally as possible.

The same goes for social settings, for example, if you're at a dinner party or an informal gathering. Control the narrative by calling out lies but don't offer any additional information. Simply request privacy and discretion as you handle your affairs. You may want to deny the truth by providing more information, but that would just feed the gossip mill, and we don't want that.

I know you may have heard this somewhere but keep it simple, short, and firm. Nothing more, nothing less. While being polite of course.

Control the narrative

Sometimes you may have to deal with a lot of disapproval from the people around you. It could be a person you greatly respect or an authority figure. No matter who they are or what they might say, it's up to you to decide whether you want to listen to them or internalize their advice.

Sometimes, these people have their own agenda or may have been deeply invested in your relationship with your ex. This means that you may not need to take their perspective to heart. Being constantly around people expressing their regret or disappointment in your actions could make you upset and unbalanced. So don't entertain it. Depending on the social context, you can choose to tune out their advice or end the conversation. Don't be afraid to walk away if you need to.

Filtering these comments helps put you in a place of control so that you can focus on your own growth and healing. Another positive is that once people around you notice that you're not entertaining this gossip, it will most likely die down.

Focus on yourself and your future.

A great way to keep yourself distracted from the rumors is to focus on other things that can make you happier, healthier, and stronger. This will help keep you from fueling those rumors and help you stay gracious when confronted with them. Some healthy ways to distract yourself include:

- Consciously spending more time with your family and friends.

- Focusing on work and achieving your work-based goals.

- Volunteering for a cause that's important to you.

- Finding new hobbies and adopting new interests.

It's never a walk in the park, and most of it involves you putting your head down and weathering the storm while waiting for it to pass. And I can promise you that it will pass.

Handling Debts and Finances After

Realistically speaking, most people have debt, and it's very likely that you left the marriage with some debt. Most times, your finances are so tied up with your spouse's that it may be difficult to see who pays for what. We've talked about handling your finances and upping your credit score in the previous chapter, so you should also check that out.

There are a lot of factors to consider when you're deciding who pays what debt. Things like your prenuptial agreement (if there was one), your state, and who incurred the debt. Of course, the best thing to do before a divorce is to figure out who incurred what debt and try to get that debt in the name of the correct partner.

If the debt was created during the marriage, the state you live in will affect the repayment distribution. In an equitable distribution state, the court will give the repayment responsibility to the person whose name is on the debt. That means that any debt incurred in your name is yours to settle while your ex settles theirs.

Apart from equitable distribution states, community property states do not assign debt based on who incurred it. Rather they split all debts evenly in the event of a divorce. These states assume that both spouses jointly own all assets, and as such, both of them are responsible for said assets. There are nine community property states in the US, and they are California, Arizona, Texas, Washington, Idaho, Louisiana, Nevada, Wisconsin, and New Mexico. So if your spouse had a $50,000 credit card debt and you're in a community property state, the lender could pursue you to get some of the money back if your ex couldn't meet up with those payments.

The important thing here is that any debt under your name just be cleared. For instance, your credit score suffers if your ex is meant to pay a portion of a debt incurred in your name and they don't make those payments on time. So even if you take legal action against them, your credit score is still affected anyway. This means that it's important to monitor debt payments and ensure they are promptly paid.

For community property states, gifts and inheritances are not jointly owned. Now, if a house was purchased in the name of a single spouse, the other spouse is still a legal co-owner, even if their name isn't on the deed.

To avoid getting stuck with debts that aren't yours, get the debt in the name of the responsible partner before the divorce is finalized. It requires your partner's cooperation, and that may not be guaranteed. If you have a mortgage or car loan, try to get it refinanced to the person who's keeping the asset before the divorce is completed. If it's already been completed, it may be possible to show the lender the divorce decree that states that your spouse is responsible for the payment, not you. The lender may allow you to strike your name off the loan and replace it with your ex's name.

You may have to consolidate credit card debts into a single debt for a lower interest rate and better repayment terms. Another option for mortgage or car loans is to sell the asset and use the cash made to service the loans.

Financial situations may be sticky but having a clear plan of action will help. A checklist like this will help:

- Take stock of your financial situation post-divorce. Do you have new bank accounts? Do you have new debts to service? List them out.

- Set up reminders and automatic repayments so your bills are paid on time.

- Portion your income such that you get to pay at least a part of your debts each month. Determine the most important debt to pay first or if it's best to pay fractionally. Speaking to a financial analyst or expert for the best advice is important.

- Make sure your name is removed from any outstanding debts you're not responsible for paying.

- If possible, sell jointly owned assets to clear off any debts.

- Maintain constant communication with your divorce attorney, especially if your ex doesn't meet up with their payments.

Sorting your debts and setting up a repayment plan is most important. Getting another stream of income may be necessary as well.

Now that you've sorted things out on the home front let's look at your children. How can you help them overcome this divorce? How can you tell if they need attention or help? What's the best way to discuss the divorce with them? Do they have to choose between you and your ex? We'll take a good look at these aspects in the next chapter.

Part Two

Protecting Yourself And Your Child

A divorce is always hard on everyone involved. More often than not, it will be brutal, torturous, and nerve-wracking. Especially on kids. A divorce from a non-narcissist partner is bad enough, but one from a narcissist is a serious challenge and is very likely to hurt your child, except you act fast. They may stop doing well in school; they may become less social than they used to be, or they can have emotional outbursts or engage in destructive behaviors.

Taking matters a step further and considering how a divorce from a narcissistic ex can affect your kid isn't something to joke about. There are so many angles to consider here. How your narc ex may have treated your child before the divorce, how they may have lashed out at the poor kid during the divorce process, and how your kid needs to cope now that you're co-parenting with them.

Truth be told, you can't afford to approach any issue that concerns your child lightly. It's possible that you may not have realized just how much damage could be done potentially, but that's why you're here.

In this part, we'll look closely at your child's emotions after the divorce. We'll examine the fact that your kid was also hurt, just like you were. We'll see how best to break the divorce news to them (if they don't already know) and even how to help them handle it afterwards for their own good. Will your child need to heal from the process, just like you?

Is it possible for you to help them get the healing they need? What if your child is torn between you and your co-parent? What then? Is there a way to handle that issue, so they don't feel like they have to choose one out of both of you? Should you consider therapy for your child? We'll address all these issues in this part.

We'll also look at practical ways to beat the narcissist at their own game. Enough with the manipulation and the games. Enough with the triggers and making you look silly all the time. You're gonna learn how to hit them where it hurts and how to walk away as the winner in your next confrontations. You're going to realize that disarming the narcissist means arming yourself – but not in the way you think. We're going to plot and plan your battle strategy like the generals of old. We're going to borrow some ancient wisdom to help you win the battle and be victorious at the end of the war. You're going to learn the best way to arm your child and protect them from your ex.

Let's get real here, is it always possible to co-parent with a narc? Are there alternatives that you can consider instead? You don't need to feel trapped or chained to your wrecking ball ex. I'll show you how to manage raising your child with them, what to expect when co-parenting with a narcissist, and how to do the best for your child at every turn.

As we go into this part, I want you to know that **you've got this.** As you go through the upcoming chapters, I want that phrase to echo in the background of your mind, your personal mantra, if you will. Think of it like the precious tank of oxygen you'd never dare to go deep sea diving without. Now that you have your oxygen let's dive in.

Chapter Four

Helping Your Children Come to Terms with Things

"Children are like wet cement. Whatever falls on them makes an impression."
—Haim Ginott

Alice had always wanted to be a mom. She loved every part of motherhood. She loved being pregnant and adored those little flutters she felt when the baby started moving to the full-on rock shows her babies used to dance to while they were in her stomach. She was a sucker for that new baby smell and that precious tight grasp with the little baby fingers. She loved watching her two girls run around and lived for their squishy hugs. Every day as she tucked them into bed, she always swore to look after them and make them happy for as long as she could.

Unfortunately, ever since she started divorce proceedings against Nate, her ex-husband, she felt she had let her babies down. She regretted everything about her marriage to him except her Amber and Mariah. She wished she knew that he was a narcissist. She wished she had spoken up earlier than she did. She wished she had done more to shield her babies from their dad. If only wishes were horses.

She noticed that her daughters were now withdrawing from her. They'd stopped giving her squishy hugs, and they didn't talk or play much anymore. When she tried to ask the girls how their visits with their dad went, Amber, her seven-year-old daughter, refused to reply while Mariah screamed "Bad Mummy!" at her and ran into her room. Alice started panicking and felt like she was losing everything that mattered to her – which was ironic because she decided to leave Nate because of her girls. But it seemed they had forgotten all the unhappiness and tears of before and now saw their father as their best friend.

To make matters worse, she didn't realize the girls were watching when she had a screaming match with Nate the other day until Mariah ran out to hug her dad protectively. It felt like the more she tried, the more everything seemed to go wrong, and she didn't know.

When she sat across from me in a small coffee shop, I could tell she was emotionally exhausted and hurting. I showed her a few of the strategies we'll look at here, and with time, she could identify Nate's tactics and arm herself against them. She was able to connect with her girls again and help them through the process. In her email to me, she said:

"I'm not 100 percent there yet, but I can definitely see a huge difference, and I'm so happy. I realize that they were really affected by the divorce, but I'm proud of the girls they're becoming, and I'm glad to be their mom."

I'll admit it; I don't know exactly what's going on with you and your co-parent. Maybe your kid started acting out in school, or they've started talking back at you and yelling at you. Maybe you suspect they're sneaking out at night whenever they're at yours. You might even be afraid that their contact with your abusive ex may permanently damage them, and you feel helpless. No matter what the situation is, there's something for you here.

Your Child Was Hurt Too

It's hard to predict how a divorce might affect your kid. Some children take the news in their stride and seem to handle it well. Others are overly concerned and may almost take it personally. Still others may take advantage of that to play their parents against each other for their own benefits. Different strokes for different folks and what not. One thing we can be sure of is the fact that your divorce does affect your child.

No matter how guilty you might feel at the moment, I want you to know that you did the right thing for yourself and your kids. Even if it doesn't seem that way sometimes, I assure you it is.

Their age is an important factor affecting how your kids respond to the divorce. Divorce affects children no matter how young they might seem. Even babies and toddlers may be aware of the divorce or the tension and may react by becoming more clingy around the parent or around new people, crying or fussing a lot when one parent is missing, or even reverting to old habits that may have been previously discarded for comfort. If your child starts to suck their thumb again, even though they broke that habit years ago, it may be a sign that they are affected by the tension in the relationship and are seeking comfort.

Children between the ages of three to five may not necessarily understand the divorce concept and may want you to get back together with your ex. They may also feel like it's their fault although things may improve with time.

Some of the ways children are affected by divorce are:

Being irritable or angry.

Some children may be so overwhelmed by separation that they may not be entirely able to express their intense emotions properly. This can manifest as anger or irritation, especially for trivial matters. They may be angry at their parents, themselves, their friends, and even their toys. If you notice that your child is always upset even after the divorce is over, it may be an extended effect of the divorce on them.

Being emotionally sensitive

We all know that divorce can trigger all sorts of emotions no matter what age we are. The same can be said of children. A child experiencing such a process can feel confused, worried, anxious, angry, or upset. The interesting thing is that they can experience all these feelings simultaneously or rapidly transition from emotion to emotion. Children need to talk to someone or express themselves to someone who can understand them and help them process their emotions.

Feeling guilty

At some point, children may blame themselves for the divorce. They might even wonder why a divorce must happen to their family, and they may think it might have something to do with them. Feeling guilty is common and can lead to issues along the line.

Falling ill more often

For some children, the stress of the divorce may affect their health, and you may find them always ill or complaining about physical pain. A lack of sleep could contribute greatly to this.

May not easily adapt to change

A child of a newly divorced couple may be forced to endure a lot of changes. It could be a change in school, a change of home, having to deal with the awareness that their parents are separated and so on. Most times, these kids may have a hard time adjusting to the changes. This can be seen as a surly, uncommunicative attitude or even tantrum, depending on the age and personality of the child.

They may start acting out

Children who have experienced divorce may engage in rebellious behavior like talking back to their parents, getting involved in fights, sneaking out, bullying, and so on. For some kids, this might be another way to express their conflicted emotions.

As difficult as it may seem for you, sometimes they may not want to share their feelings with you because they may be angry at you, especially if they feel like you initiated the divorce. The most important thing is to understand their origin and try to meet them halfway.

Helping Your Child Handle the Divorce News

How you break the news of your divorce to your child and how you and your spouse behave around your child or children may be the greatest determinant of how your child reacts to the news of a divorce.

If you're not careful, you may add more confusion than clarity to the situation. If you can, discuss this with your spouse so that you can draw up a plan of action. This may not be possible if your ex is being uncooperative. In this case, you may need to handle this yourself.

Here are a few tips to help you break the news to your child:

Plan what you're going to say ahead of time

It doesn't have to be a fancy script. It just has to be a truthful, age-appropriate way to explain your separation. Use terms they are more likely to understand but don't go into too many details.

Present it as a mutual decision

Avoid laying the blame on one person. Portray it as something that was agreed on. Even though your ex may lay the blame on you when they speak to your child later on, you mustn't apportion any blame. You can use phrases like *"Mommy and Daddy don't feel as close as they used to before,"* or *"We argue a lot, and we don't want to keep doing that."*

Inform them of any changes that may occur

The last thing you want to do is leave your kid unaware of the possible changes that may occur in the wake of the separation. Make sure you spell out the expected changes so they are not taken by surprise. For example, which parent will be moving out? Will the children have to move to another house? Will there be a change in their routine?

Try to answer these questions as clearly as possible.

Let them know it's not their fault

We've already established that some kids may feel misplaced guilt and blame themselves for the divorce. Be very clear that it's not their fault. Also, reassure them that this doesn't mean you've stopped loving them less or that their other parent loves them any less. Try to stay calm and cheerful because your children will take their emotional cues from you. If you seem sad and depressed, they will most likely be afraid and sad as well.

Give your kids a chance to speak

Now that you've explained everything to them, give them a chance to speak. Reassure them that you won't judge them for any of their reactions. Also, tell them they won't hurt your feelings no matter what they say. If they seem sad or angry, don't be too quick to cheer them up. Allow them to experience their emotions. Ask them to tell you more about their feelings and try to understand what they're saying. Ensure that you provide a safe space where they can talk about their true feelings. Note that you might have to repeat this talk a couple more times because your kids may still have something else to say later.

Above all, honesty and a sense of calm are the most important things you need when discussing the divorce with your kids. Tell them all at once rather than letting them hear from a sibling. This is not the time to get so wrapped up in arranging your life post-divorce that you forget to pay attention to your children.

How To Discuss Your Divorce With Your Kids

There are different approaches to discussing divorce depending on your child's age. Before we get into the best ways to discuss your separation with your kids based on their ages, know that you can minimize the tension your children may feel concerning this divorce.

I can almost hear you asking how that is possible. Simple. Make their well-being your topmost priority. Be patient, be willing to listen, and constantly reassure your kids. Don't let go of old routines because of the divorce. If you have to, simply modify the existing routines to fit your new situation so that they still have some familiar structures around them. This shows them that there is still stability in their lives, come what may.

If possible, be as cordial and polite with your ex as much as possible. No matter whatever harm or abuse your former spouse may have caused you, seeing both parents in conflict is disturbing for your kids, so spare them that sight as much as possible.

Your kids would preferably want both their parents to be still involved in their lives. They would also appreciate it if you seemed to get along well with your ex. If you have many open disagreements and confrontations, especially about them, they may start to feel guilty and assume that they are the cause of the divorce.

Ages 0-5 years

When talking to kids between the ages of 0 to 5 years, use simple, understandable terms. Children under the age of 3 years do not understand complex situations, events or feelings while those between ages 3 to 5 years are quite dependent but also have some streaks of independence. They also see the world as it revolves around them and may be unable to distinguish between real life and fantasy. They may not have the right idea about the divorce and may think that the parent that moved out left them. They may need to be told over and over again in simple terms about the divorce.

Children of this age range may react to the news by expressing fear or anger about that situation or other situations. They may also become more anxious and clingy.

To help your child in this age range adjust well, you need to ensure that they are consistently cared for in the same way they're used to. A sense of love and stability is very important.

Here's a short list to guide your conversation with your toddler:

- Do it together. If possible, let both parents be present so there's a united front that shows stability.

- Speak in simple terms. Use words that your kid will understand. Have all the necessary information about living arrangements, custody, and visitation arrangements. If your child has witnessed some arguments, acknowledge them and say that this step is best for the family.

- Reassure your kid that it's not their fault, and do not assign blame to either parent. Don't give any details; just keep it simple and short.

A good example is, *"Mommy and Daddy are going to live apart, but we'll always be your mommy and daddy, and we'll always love you."*

Get ready to answer their questions and repeat this talk in the future.

Ages 6-9 years

If your kids are between the ages of 6 and 9, they can understand what's going on around them, but they may not be able to handle the complex divorce aspects. They may have more friends and have developed more relationships at home. Some may be fixated on reuniting their parents, which may stop them from healing properly. They may also try to blame the divorce on a specific action; for example, they may think it happened because of an argument or one person did something another person didn't like.

They may react by being rude, talking about getting their parents together, or expressing anger. Fights and tantrums are not uncommon as well.

When breaking the news to your child:

- Pick a good time when both parents are available.

- Speak about the divorce in simple terms.

- Inform them about the changes and reassure them that both parents still love them.

- Encourage them to ask questions or talk about their feelings.

- Books about divorce may be helpful here as well.

Maintain familiar routines with your children as much as possible and encourage them to speak up if they can.

Ages 10-12 Years

Children in this age range have a better-developed understanding and can think and talk about the circumstances related to divorce to some extent. They also place a lot of value on their relationships outside the home, such as with their teachers, friends, etc.

They may think you're leaving them or blame the divorce on one parent. They may pick sides and classify a parent as good and the other as bad. They may express their anger by lashing out at their parents, fighting with schoolmates, or being generally irritable. They may also have physical symptoms like headaches or an upset stomach often.

Some tips to help when talking to your child:

- Be more direct because children of this age can understand feelings better.

- Be clear that it's a mutual decision, and don't blame a particular parent.

- Encourage them to ask questions by saying things like, *"Most kids aren't happy to hear that their parents are divorcing; it's OK if you're angry."*

- Don't forget that they could be stressed or anxious, so be sure to address all possible sources of stress

Teenagers

Early teens (13-16 years)

Children in this age bracket are even better able to comprehend issues about the divorce. You can engage them in discussions, and they are likely to ask questions to increase their understanding.

They are also in that phase where they question parental authority and desire much more independence. They may have noticed signs of tension between you and your ex and may not be surprised.

Teens in this age range may also often be sulky or moody, so it may not be easy to ascertain if divorce is a factor. It's best to keep a close eye on them for any changes that may manifest after the divorce. They could also be rude, confrontational, or even more so after the divorce.

When breaking the news to them:

- Keep it simple and explain that you'll be better off separated from the other parent.

- Just because they are more likely to understand the complexities of the divorce doesn't mean you should tell them dirty details or overshare.

- Explain the expected changes to them and the reasons behind them.

- They may be more concerned with their social life than anything else, so if you can allay their fears and anxieties about the changes, go ahead.

Older teens (17-19 years)

It may be easy to assume that children in this category are practically adults and are better equipped to understand the nuances of the divorce, but a study has shown that children who were very young when their parents divorced were less psychologically affected than their older siblings. Older children were seen to have more stressful memories of the divorce (Wallerstein, 2014).

Older teenagers are in a better position to understand divorce and most likely know other teens with divorced parents. They may already have an idea about the issues going on and may even see the divorce as a relief.

They may not feel like they are at fault or want their parents to stay together. They are also more likely to accept the divorce and may be more concerned about its impact on their social life

This doesn't mean that they aren't distressed or traumatized about the situation; they're just less likely to show it or discuss it with you. They may react strongly or throw a tantrum. They may become distant and want to be left alone. They may also be more rebellious than usual and try to test your limits. This is the time to be firm but loving.

When breaking the news to your teen:

- Explain the situation in simple terms without a lot of details.

- Explain the new arrangements and expected changes.

- Reassure them that you still love them and that you'll be present in their lives.

- Be prepared for a strong reaction or concern about their lives, especially if they have to move or change schools.

- Give them space to process their feelings about the situation, and don't push them to talk too soon.

- Even if they claim they don't want to talk or be around you, try to spend time with them to show them that you're always there for them.

Try to present a united front in front of your children. Reassure them as much as possible. Encourage them to speak with you to say what's on their minds. It may be an uphill battle, but you'll get there eventually.

Common Questions Your Kids are Likely to Ask (And Appropriate Answers to Give)

While you're working through your divorce, your kids will have a lot of questions. Below are some common ones and samples of appropriate answers you can give.

Question: What did I do wrong?

Answer: This is a type of question that can come from kids 11 and up, especially teenagers. You need to assure your kids that none of it is their fault. "Honey, this is between your dad and me. It has nothing to do with you. We love you, and you're a huge blessing to us," you might answer.

Question: Will you be getting back together?

Answer: If you're not doing a trial separation, you need to let your kids know that you're going your separate ways. Raising their hopes may hurt them afresh from time to time and eventually slow their healing process.

Question: What do I tell my friends?

Answer: If your kid is worried about what their friends will think, assure your kid that the divorce is you and your ex's decision and that one's parents are getting divorced doesn't mean friendships should be destroyed or that their friends should think less of them. Promise them that true friends won't judge or hate them because of the divorce situation and that their friends are probably going through the same things.

Question: Will Daddy ever come visiting?

Answer: If your husband or wife will be visiting, explain the arrangement to your kid, and if not, explain that too.

Question: Is Mommy a bad person? (Or Daddy, depending on who isn't taking custody)

Answer: Remember never to badmouth your ex to your child. For older children, you can face facts and tell them that things aren't working out but avoid statements like "Your mom's pure evil," or "Your dad is sick in the head," when you can simply be nice and maintain your cool.

Question: Will you leave me too if I do something bad?

Answer: This is a valid question, and how you answer it is very important. This is where you assure your kid that divorce isn't something nice and that you hope never to have to go through it again. Assure them of your unconditional love and tell them that you'll always be there for them.

Question: Do you still love Daddy?

Answer: Answer "Yes, I do," but it's a different kind of love now, more like the one good friends share.

Question: Will you marry someone else?

Answer: "Maybe, but only with your approval." Your kid will want to know that they'll always be a priority to you, so assure them of this repeatedly.

Helping Your Kids Heal From the Emotional Abuse You All Went Through

Now, let's bring it home, the odds that your kid has been emotionally abused by your narc partner are higher than usual. In the US, 36% of reported child abuse cases had emotional abuse as a major identified factor (Nguyen-Feng, 2020).

Another report stated that at least 2.3% of children in the United States experience emotional abuse in a year (US Administration for Children and Families). Unfortunately, emotional abuse isn't reported as frequently as physical or sexual abuse. This is because, most times, it is difficult to detect. It can be gradual and discreet, slowly attacking the child's self-esteem. Many children would not report emotional abuse because they mostly can't identify it, and they've normalized abusive behavior.

Emotional abuse leaves the victim feeling shame, fear, confusion, isolation, and neglect. It can occur in different varied forms. It may manifest as insults and deliberate attempts to demean the child in public. Emotional neglect and abandonment are also forms of emotional abuse.

Parents who place heavy emotional burdens on their children are also guilty of emotional abuse. This could look like telling them unnecessary details and facts that may be too weighty for them to comprehend. It could be telling them to do something inappropriate like stealing, lying to the police, or lying in court. Parents who punish their children harshly such that the punishment far outweighs the crime are also emotionally abusing their children.

You need to look out for the signs of possible emotional abuse in your kids. Some signs you could start looking out for are:

- Being anxious all the time

- Poor academic performance

- Self-harm or a desire to cut themselves

- Negative self-talk.

- Disproportionately afraid of a parent or a guardian.

- Reverting to former habits for comfort. For example, they may start sucking their lips or even sucking their thumb.

- Not wanting to socialize as much as before.

- Being clingy or trying to seek attention from the abuser or the other parent.

- Low self-esteem.

- Frequent headaches and stomach aches.

- Running away from home or avoiding home.

Some risk factors may indicate if a parent or guardian abuses a child emotionally. The presence of some of these factors does not mean that emotional abuse is happening, but the fact they exist shows a high possibility that emotional abuse may go on. Some of these factors are:

- Being abused as a child

- Alcohol or the use of drugs

- Being physically or mentally ill

- Being isolated socially or even separated from extended family

- Divorce

Helping Your Children Come to Terms with Things

- Financial stress, as well as poverty or unemployment

- Domestic abuse

If your partner or spouse has experienced any of these risk factors, it's possible that they may be emotionally abusing your child or that they may have emotionally abused them.

Now that you've identified some signs that your child has definitely been emotionally abused and that your partner has abused them in one way or the other, there are some steps you can take to help your child recover from this abuse.

1. Create a safe space for your child

The first step to helping your child heal from emotional abuse is to create a space where they can feel safe and secure. Here, they can express their feelings without fear or judgment from you or anyone. A great way to get them to open up might be to share some age-appropriate ways you overcame bullying yourself or something similar. Don't tiptoe around it or try to downplay it. They've had a bad thing happen to them, and you need to let them know that you're there for them and can handle whatever they have to say.

Your child may not feel safe enough to talk initially, but with time and the demonstration that they can trust you, they will eventually start to open up to you. Try not to put too much pressure on them in the meantime.

2. Writing may help

If your child is old enough to write, a journal where they can write how they feel will be super helpful. This will help them when they are emotionally distressed and can serve as a safe outlet for processing their distress. Some prompts that may get them started are:

- How do you feel right now?

- What was the best part of your week? Why?

- What was the worst part of your week? Why?

- What are some things that make you feel good?

- What are the things that hurt your feelings?

These simple prompts are sufficient to help your child start writing again if they need to.

Therapy may also be of great benefit to your child. The key to helping them heal is to be loving, consistent, and encouraging. Keep telling and showing them they are valued. Help them to remember that the actions of the abuser do not define them.

When Your Child is Experiencing Loyalty Conflicts

Your children are used to seeing you and your partner happy. They may assume that you are both meant to be together, no matter what. Being exposed to the strong conflict between their parents may be distressing to your child. If there were long court disputes during the process, your child might be inclined to pick one parent at the detriment of the other.

Now, it's entirely possible that your child may already have a favorite parent. Some children just have a special attachment to that one parent. But on the whole, they naturally have a sense of devotion and attachment to their parents, and that's the same thing as loyalty. When a divorce happens, a loyalty conflict might arise. Your child may feel like they have to choose between one parent and the other. Or worse still,

Helping Your Children Come to Terms with Things

and this is a typical narc tactic, your co-parent may give the child everything they want – the latest devices, maybe a car, sweets, and ice cream, or whatever catches their fancy. Even doing things like letting them go out for parties on school nights or staying up past their bedtime may make the kids like the other parent and want to spend more time with them.

If there's a stepparent in the picture, your child may not take to them easily. They may feel like they're being disloyal to the other parent, which could also lead to a loyalty conflict.

A child who's experiencing a loyalty conflict may be anxious about spending time with the other parent or may become withdrawn when it's time to leave. They may cry, have headaches, or throw tantrums. They may not want to see the other parent at all, or they may not want to talk about the other parent in front of you. They may subtly criticize the other parent by talking down on their time with them or rolling their eyes when they're referring to the other parent.

If you're not the favorite parent in this scenario, that is, if your child has a stronger attachment to the other parent, you may notice that they are sullen and withdrawn around you. If the other parent says the child was happy while they were with them, that could be a sign to take note of. Sometimes, your child may lie about their experience in the other parent's home and pretend like they didn't have fun or enjoy spending time with the other parent, especially if there is a stepparent in the picture. They may feel guilty and think they're protecting you.

One thing that could make loyalty conflicts worse is visibly fighting in front of your children. Doing things like bad-mouthing the other parent's attitudes, decisions, new partner, and activities will set off loyalty conflicts or make them worse. Instead, aim to maintain a polite and maybe even cordial relationship with your ex, if possible. If it's not possible, avoid being around them as much as you can.

Let your child know they can feel comfortable with their parents and having fun with the other parent would not hurt your feelings. Reassure them and help them understand that being loyal to one parent over the other isn't necessary. It might be best to encourage your child to spend more time with the other parent.

How Loyalty Conflicts Can Impact Your Child

Let's be honest, sometimes a loyalty conflict doesn't really sound all that bad. Especially when you're the favorite parent and your child isn't really into your ex anymore. Bonus points if your ex is a narc and your child is better off without interacting with them anymore, right? I mean, what's not to love about it? You can be sure your child won't want to spend extra time with your ex and that they'd always give you the 411 on what's happening at the other parent's house. You may even feel like you can confide in your kid a little about what they did to you so that your kid won't turn out like them. Plus, the emotional boost that comes with knowing that your kid puts you first and chooses you every single time is second to none.

So you find yourself subtly trying to make them even more loyal to you; you let your kid overhear them being mean to you, or you talk about sensitive issues when you know that you can be overheard. You encourage your child to bad mouth the other parent, maybe not in an obvious way, but you don't stop them either when they say nasty things about them. You may even spoil your kid a little by giving them whatever they want, all so that your home is more welcoming and comfortable for them. After all, they're your kids, and you're not the bad person here, right? You're just a mom or a dad who wants the best for their child. If that means showing them who the other person truly is or using some subtle tactics to win them over, so be it. All's fair in love and war, right?

Wrong.

Now, I'm not condemning you here. Because, trust me, that parental protective urge is strong. I mean, if it has moms lifting cars off their babies to save them, it sure as shooting can push you to skew the odds in your favor, and for seemingly good reasons too. It's love, and in these uncertain times post-divorce, you need to look out for your kids. I won't argue with you, but I'd ask that we take a look at how this conflict can affect your children.

Generally, children who have experienced a divorce don't have the best time of it. They are often anxious and depressed; in fact, a connection between divorce and poor academic performance in kids has been established (Potter 2010).

Feeling like they need to choose a side can be extremely stressful for your child, especially if you discuss all the underlying issues in the marriage with your child and unconsciously (or consciously) encourage them to take your side. Fighting about your child in front of your child can be upsetting for them to witness and will do more harm than good. If you throw a step-parent or a new boyfriend or girlfriend into the mix, it makes it worse for your kids because they feel like they can't like the new person or get to know them. This could either be because they resent the new person for worsening the separation between parents or even because they feel like one parent is cheating on the other, even though they are divorced.

Another important point of concern for your child may be that both parents may not seem capable of taking care of them. Think about it, if you can't get along well with your ex, what's to say both of you could put yourselves together well enough to be good parents to your child? I don't know about you, but that thought would make me very anxious and feel insecure. How much more your kid, who's probably experienced the most trauma, thanks to the divorce, and needs all the stability and love they can get?

Many parents forget that their kid is always watching and listening, especially when it doesn't seem like they are. So, on the one hand, you have kids who don't think their parents can keep it together long enough to be good parents, or they may even feel like their parents are being self-centered and probably don't care about them anymore, and on the other hand, you have parents who are probably too caught up in wrestling with their ex to realize that their kids need help. That's a disaster in the making if you ask me. I wouldn't be surprised to see that your kids may start to act out, be rude to you, talk back at you, sneak out of the house or play both of you against each other just because they can. They could also be withdrawn and sulky, choosing not to talk to either of their parents and instead spend time with other family members and friends.

Now let's take a glimpse as to how this conflict can affect their own relationships in the future. Studies have shown that children who have experienced divorce are more likely to engage in risky sexual activity at younger ages, experience non-marital childbirth, cohabitation, early marriages, discord, and eventually divorce later in life (Donofrio, 2011).

Experiencing divorce spiked with lots of conflicts, especially at a young age, may leave children with the impression that most marriages end in divorce and that there's no point in getting married in the first place. They may also learn that lying, manipulation, and confrontation should be the order of the day in their future relationships. In essence, your child may never learn how to have a healthy, adult relationship because they never saw one.

I know this sounds scary, but it just means that you need to sit up and take charge of your interactions with your ex as well as your relationship with your children.

Is Therapy Necessary For The Kid?

I get this question all the time, and it's very valid. Overall, going through a divorce is super stressful for kids in so many ways. Experiencing a lot of conflicting emotions about the new changes in their lives, comparing their parents to other parents who are still together, and maybe even getting stigmatized by other kids at school because of the divorce are just a few things that could make a divorce unbearable for your kid.

One angle to children experiencing a divorce is the genuineness of their reactions. It's perfectly normal to expect some change in your child, no matter how young they are. This is because a divorce is not a walk in the park, and so they'll need to deal with a lot of stuff every day. Your child acting out means they feel safe enough to express their true feelings about the situation. This is good because that means they're working through it, to some extent, and that at least those emotions aren't bottled up within.

The reverse would be the case if your kid doesn't show much of anything, and it can be because they feel like you may not be able to handle that. They could be considering your own emotions, especially if they're aware that you've been abused, to the detriment of their own emotions. So, if your child is rude or cries more than usual, it's not really a bad thing; it just shows that they are processing the situation.

Deciding how to handle your child's new behavior may leave you confused but for the most part, let them know that you understand that it's a difficult time for them and that you care about their feelings, and you're ready to talk about anything with them at every point in time. It's important not to push them to discuss it but just casually bring it up from time to time as naturally as possible. They may not respond to your cues immediately, but you can bet that they're listening.

In general, your kid may not need therapy because they're bound to experience the effects of the stress associated with the divorce. However, there are a few pointers that may indicate that therapy may be beneficial for them. Some of them are:

- If your child asks to see a therapist. May not happen often, but it's possible.

- If your child's behavior like crying excessively, anger, or withdrawal persists over a long time (several months).

- If your child's behavior affects their normal activities or the normal functioning of the family.

- If teachers, relatives, or close friends are concerned about your kid's new changes.

- An obvious change in eating habits that cannot be explained medically.

- Frequent complaints of headaches or stomach aches.

- If your child constantly complains of feeling tired or uninterested in the usual things.

- Poor academic performance.

- A new lack of interest in socializing as usual.

- New intrusive fears and phobias like separation anxiety in young children.

Speaking privately to an expert or a counselor may also shed some light and help you decide if you need to take your child to therapy.

If you decide they need therapy, refrain from making it look like they're not normal or need help. Instead, you could go together as a family,

Helping Your Children Come to Terms with Things

allowing private sessions with your child and the therapist at any point necessary. Yes, the possible effects of divorce on your kids may look scary. But being committed to their well-being and practicing everything we've discussed here will help.

Now, let's talk about your narcissist ex and how to successfully survive this co-parenting phase without losing your dignity or sanity.

Chapter Five

Disarming The Narcissist

> "If you hold on to hurt and anger with a narcissist, the children will have no normal parent. The narcissistic parent will use them as puppets, love bomb, and abandon them. You are their only hope."
> — Tracy Malone

Here's a hill I'm willing to defend to the last man. In fact, someone I know has described it as a tune I could sing about forever and dance alone to. He's not wrong.

So here it is: disarming a narcissist is all about you, not them. I'll say it again because the second time is always the charm. Disarming a narcissist is all about you and definitely not about them. I'm looking to get these words printed on T-shirts, mugs, and caps; that's how important they are. This is because those words hold the key to understanding the principle that'll lead you to victory in this battle against the narcissist. And to defeat your enemy, you must first defeat yourself. I know, I know, I sound like Sun Tzu, but it's the truth.

What do I mean? I mean that disabling the narcissist's devices and undermining their stronghold starts with you. How? Because it is you. The narcissist is empty and full of fear. This is why they try to get their validation and adoration from people around them. They are trying to fill that bottomless hole within them that demands that they control and diminish people to seem powerful. How do they get their fill? From you. Your reactions, your tears, your despair, and your anger. What about that moment when you flared up and had a massive argument with them in public? That's their supply. Knowing that you looked a little crazy because they seemed innocent during the whole incident? Icing on the cake for them.

If you're hearing me, and I know you are, you'll see that this means that the narcissist enjoys controlling and manipulating you. They take satisfaction in demeaning you and making you lose yourself repeatedly. Because they feed off your reactions in scenarios like that. They take pride in knowing that you're a puppet attached to their strings. There's not much they wouldn't do to keep it that way.

Now that you know this information and how critical you are to their operations, what next? It's simple. You cut off their supply. You take yourself out of the equation. That's the basic concept.

We're going to see exactly how you can achieve that with your narcissist co-parent and how to come out victorious after every confrontation you'll have with them.

A note of warning – this isn't a walk in the park, and you'll have to do a lot of inner work. But the rewards far outweigh the costs, and I don't know about you, but I love deals like that.

If you feel the urge to sing this tune with me and do a little jig while we're at it, I wouldn't say no. Heck, I appreciate the company.

The Psychology of the Narcissist

"It is in the roots, not the branches, that a tree's greatest strength lies."—Matshona Dhliwayo.

Before we can talk about gaining victory and freedom from a narcissist, I'd like to ask you a question.

Let's say you work for a marketing company and were assigned to prepare a pitch to a big prospective who other companies like yours are currently wooing. What would you do?

Before you prepare your pitch, you would need to do a lot of research, right? You need to know exactly what those other companies are offering your client and how you can one-up them. With that knowledge in hand, you can be sure to create the best pitch possible and land the client easy peasy.

That's the same principle we're going to apply here. We need to do a little research to see what makes a narcissist well, a narcissist. What makes them tick? Why do they behave the way they do? Finding this out is like uprooting a tree entirely instead of cutting it. Effective and final with no chances of regrowth. Studying the narcissist will help you craft strategies that will put them down once and for all.

So narcissism is the hallmark of Narcissistic Personality Disorder (NPD), which is a mental disorder where people have an almost obsessive need for attention and admiration coupled with an overblown sense of self. A third and important characteristic is that, oftentimes, they lack empathy for others as well.

At the core of the narcissist is a fragile self-esteem and fear, which drives their behavior. Getting everyone's attention and adulation affirms the fact that they are truly as important as they think they are, and this reassures that inner part of them that's scared that they are worthless.

Because they don't have much empathy, they have no issues with soothing their fragile egos by putting other people down.

So a narcissist is like a Russian doll with several layers of domineering arrogant beliefs and behaviors, which may lead you to expect that they have a giant sense of self-confidence, but alas, once you get to the middle, you'll find a pathetic, small version of themselves.

Someone with NPD may have all or some of these characteristics:

- A huge sense of entitlement to special treatment and privileges even if they don't deserve them.

- The ability to take advantage of others for their own benefit without remorse.

- An obsession with fantasies of power, success, beauty, brilliance, influence, or the perfect partner.

- The belief that they are better than others and a need for constant praise and admiration.

- The inability to understand or recognize other people's needs.

- Being overly critical about everyone and everything – no one can be as perfect as they are.

- The tendency to exaggerate their achievements so they are larger than life.

- The inability to entertain or handle criticism of any kind, which may make them irrationally angry or impatient, or they could be withdrawn as well. They have a penchant for revenge if they feel they've been wronged or criticized.

Of course, there's a difference between someone with NPD and someone who only exhibits narcissistic traits. People with NPD have the whole complex going on for them, and they tend to express intense signs of narcissism. These signs are so intense that they negatively affect their daily life. This is what qualifies it as a personality disorder.

Whereas people that only have narcissistic behavior may not exhibit all the behaviors, and it may not be as severe as those with NPD. Unfortunately, it might not be easy to place who has what. Also, upbringing directly influences the presence and intensity of narcissistic traits.

Someone with NPD will intentionally become toxic to others and exploit other people constantly to further their own agendas. They will constantly lie, make themselves look good and others look bad, and deceive everyone for their own purposes. Sometimes, it may not even be for an obvious benefit; they may just enjoy manipulation and deception for its own sake.

This means that narcissism exists on a spectrum from mild to very intense. A true narcissist finds it difficult to understand the concept of love because they lack the empathy needed. For them, all relationships are more transactional than anything. The end goal is to make themselves feel better, and they don't mind exchanging attention and a similitude of love to achieve that. Unfortunately, as the relationship advances, there's an increased demand for more commitment and a deeper level of intimacy. And that's where the facade dissolves. They can only fake it for so long.

The word 'narcissism' is getting more popular every day and gaining a lot of traction, but most people don't fully grasp what it truly means. It goes beyond a deep sense of self-love and entitlement to a lack of empathy and a drive to seek validation in whatever manner the narc deems fit.

Most people with NPD or people who exhibit narcissist traits rarely believe they have a problem. If they do admit that they are narcissistic, they tend to see it as an achievement or a positive thing instead of a problem.

Riddle me this, how can you solve a problem if you don't even admit you have one? Exactly. You can't.

Notice how we didn't talk about how other people can affect the narcissist and how they behave? That's because it's all about them. So you're not the cause of the problem. But the solution to the problem lies with you. Let's see how we can do this.

Setting Boundaries With a Narcissist

"Knowing yourself is the beginning of all wisdom. "- Aristotle

Someone I was privileged to talk with while he was going through the ordeal of co-parenting said this to me once, and I believe it's very valid here.

"I learnt the hard way that if you want to beat the narcissist at their own game and come out as the winner, you have to first of all realize that you deserve to win. You have to feel worthy of being a winner."

You have to throw that belief that you don't deserve to win. That guilt that makes you think you still deserve to be tormented by your ex because you didn't realize their real personality is gonna have to go out the door too. You'll have to sit with yourself and teach yourself to realize that you deserve more. You deserve true happiness, and you deserve to take yourself back from the narc.

You can achieve this by setting boundaries. Setting boundaries is the best way to handle a narcissist. Co-parenting with a narc may turn out to be worse than being married to them, especially if you approach it with the same mindset that you did while you were married to them.

Your child presents a wide-open doorway for them to march into your life and make it as miserable as they possibly can.

Here's how to set effective boundaries with a narcissist

Arm yourself.

This sounds dramatic and calls to mind a scene from ancient times, maybe Sparta, where the soldiers picked up the necessary weapons from the armory in a very systematic manner. Well, we're gonna be doing something like that here too.

Arming yourself means realizing that you're not who the narcissist says you are, that you're responsible for your own choices and that you're capable of doing what's best for you. Whew, sounds like a lot, but stay with me here.

Narcissists thrive on control and deception. A huge part of that means that you've been subconsciously made to see yourself in a certain way that helps the narc achieve what they want. Usually, this is a demeaning thought or belief you may have accepted. Interestingly, narcs tend to project their own negative tendencies on others. Think about it. It certainly explains why your ex was so suspicious of you cheating when, in fact, they were cheating all this time.

Unfortunately, this means that their victims tend to accept these narratives hook, line, and sinker. So today, remind yourself that you're not defined by whatever your ex said you were or insinuated you were. You have to reject any negativity and only choose to view yourself in a positive light.

A question I get a lot at this point is this "*But there's cold hard evidence that I'm selfish/lazy/careless, etc. I've shown these behaviors over and over again. How can I forgive myself and move on from this?*"

Give yourself grace.

That's it. Give yourself grace. I don't know about you but choosing to judge myself based on past actions when I could potentially do better in the future looks like a stinky deal to me, and I would not touch it with a ten-foot pole. You shouldn't either.

Realizing that you're the one responsible for your own choices can be a bit of a culture shock, especially if you've spent a lot of time with the narc, but you need to get to that point. You have to stop thinking that you can't help yourself whenever your ex says something. You have to realize that you can choose to walk away instead of engaging in a fight or showing your emotions. You can make a choice. You're not automatically controlled by them. You never were, and you sure as shooting aren't now. You have to take your power and agency back from the narc. This will come in handy when setting these boundaries.

The average narc works by eroding your self-trust and self-esteem so that you rely on them for validation and direction. Cultivating the habit of trusting yourself to make the best choices for you and your kids won't come easy to you. I'm not even gonna sugarcoat it. But as always, it has to be done. Again, give yourself grace. You can and will make mistakes, but those can be handled privately by you. They're certainly not the end of the world. You'll learn from the mistakes and move forward.

See how it all comes together?

Limit your conversations

Again, choosing to communicate only via email is a great way to ensure you're in control of the situation. This helps to reduce conflict and eliminate any potential drama that face-to-face conflict may cause. This will even help your kids avoid witnessing conflict between the two of you entirely. That's one less source of stress for them.

My phone is indispensable to me, and I'm sure yours is too. But thanks to all the modes of communication available now, being too available is a problem. This may not have occurred to you before but limiting contact helps a lot. All you need to do is set up an email address to communicate with your ex, set up a phone number where they can reach the kids if they need to, and maybe an emergency contact if necessary. This contact can be a trusted person who's able to assess any so-called emergencies, act in your stead, or contact you if need be.

That's it. That's all you need. Bear in mind that they can become increasingly aggressive, especially if they realize that you're trying to limit contact with them. Just keep firm to this boundary, and you'll eventually triumph.

Set boundaries around your home.

Stop letting your ex into your house. This may not be obvious, especially if you once shared that home, but it needs to stop. Don't let them bring their drama and conflict into it. Instead, change the locks, ensure drop-offs and pickups are outside the house or in a neutral location like a school or a park, and keep it that way. Do not let them get familiar with your home. They no longer have that right.

Set boundaries for your kids too.

You may feel the urge to relax your previous rules with your children because they may be going through a lot but don't. You're most likely the only parent who can enforce some form of stability and structure for your kids. So keep enforcing those rules whenever they're with you. Even if they claim they don't do that in the other parent's house, stand firm.

You also need to limit contact with your kids when they're at your ex's place. This is because they may be unknowingly passing on information that could trigger you. Explain to them that they need to contact you only in times of emergencies. In the same vein, try not to allow your ex to interact with your children too much while they're with you. It may sound selfish, but it's necessary. Your time with your kids is sacrosanct and should be treated as such.

Your ex may most likely see your kids as an extension of themselves and try to control them. This is typical narc behavior. Teach your kids to be independent and self-sufficient. Teach them to have a sense of individuality. You're probably the only one who'll be doing it. Teach them to be emotionally intelligent and socially adept too. It's a lot of work, but it needs to be done.

Stand firm

When you have to deal with your ex face to face, stand firm and reinforce your boundaries. Don't be aggressive, sarcastic, or demeaning. Nope, that's not the way. Instead, be polite, assertive, and show no emotions. If they start criticizing you, instead of fighting back and defending yourself, simply hang up the phone, end the conversation or leave their vicinity. Do this as unemotionally as possible. Eventually, they'll learn that you're serious about your boundaries, realize that you'll no longer humor them, and hopefully move on to another supply.

Never admit to making a mistake. Simply stay friendly, brief, informative, and firm. Always keep records of whatever happens between you. Missed payments? Write it down with proof. Didn't show up for visitation? Write it. As trivial as they may seem, everything will come in handy if you ever have to go back to court.

In a nutshell, limiting contact with your ex and being responsible for your children is the bedrock of co-parenting with a narc.

It's tough but necessary.

How to Keep Calm When They are Infuriating

I'll just burst your bubble before we go much further here. I'm not giving any hack or magic trick for staying calm when facing a narcissist. I'm not even promising you that you'll be able to stay calm when your narc ex is infuriating at first. It's not easy, and remember that grace we spoke about earlier? I'll need you to take some more of it again for yourself.

I say this because whenever people hear that I'm speaking about this topic, they get excited and think I'm about to perform magic. But no.

I mean, if you look at it critically, you'll see that your behavioral patterns whenever you engage with your ex have become a habit now. Your brain is wired to react that way because you've done it repeatedly. That's a strong habit, and it won't disappear in one day or maybe even one year. So, you're used to being drawn into a blowout argument whenever you engage with them, or you probably leave feeling like crap thanks to their acerbic tongue, or maybe your routine is to cry after you talk to them. Whatever it is, hear me now – it's not gonna disappear, and it's not gonna be easy.

But the good news is that it's possible, and it will happen faster than you expect. That's a silver lining, right?

The first step is just building on what we already talked about before. It's about finding, choosing, and loving yourself. It's about pulling down any ideas about yourself that may have taken root in your mind, thanks to them. It's a lot of self-reflection and inner work, but it's been done, and it will be done again. By you.

Two practical ways to do this are:

Reflecting on your wounds

Examine the content of your previous confrontations. What point do they make that seems to get you every time? Write them down.

Healing yourself with love

Now write down responses you would give if your youngest child said something similar about themselves or your best friend said something similar. Now say those responses to yourself with as much love and care as you can. Make them your words of affirmation and write them everywhere you can.

That's it. You can and should do this as much as possible. Once you have that down pat, you're ready.

Here are my three quick tips to stay ice cool when your narc is trying to get your goat:

1. Take a mental step back

Armed with your words of affirmation, take a step back and realize that this whole situation has been devised to upset you. Strongly tell yourself not to play into their hands. Instead, think of your favorite place or favorite thing to do. For some people I've spoken to, a personal favorite is them imagining their ex being humiliated in public. Whatever floats your boat.

Anyway, picture yourself in your favorite place. The point is to keep your power and control. You may even tune them out and focus entirely on your happy place.

2. Show no emotions and maintain previously set boundaries

This may sound tough, but it's very important. Showing no emotion means that you're depriving the narcissist of their supply. Be as emotionless as possible and restate your boundaries.

It could sound like, "I've informed you that I won't tolerate you raising your voice at me anymore. If you're not ready to have a civil discussion right now, we can pick this up later."

Reinforcing your boundaries is a great way to regain control.

3. Leave

If they escalate or they're not relenting, then you have to leave. Cut the call, slam the door in their face or leave the premises. Don't threaten to leave; don't change your mind once you've taken the first step to leave. Strengthen your resolve and leave. Do it decisively without looking back. It's not a sign of defeat or cowardice; rather, it's a victory for you. You've managed to deprive the narc of their supply, and you've had the last word by leaving. Sounds like a win-win to me. Practicing this won't be easy by any stretch, and you may not be able to do all three steps successfully. Give yourself grace. You've got this.

Arming Yourself Against The Narcissist

Now it's time to get down and dirty. Engaging with a narcissist is something that has to be carefully considered and planned.

Did someone say it sounds like we're planning to win a battle? Yeah, this is a full-on battle, and no war is won without a strategy. The previous sections have been about preparing you for your next encounter with them, and this is where everything comes together.

Here's how to come out victorious the next time you have to face your narc ex:

Know what type of narcissist you're handling

We all know that narcissists are insecure, too sensitive, and do not really like themselves. This is what drives their behavior. But more than that, there are subtypes of narcissists.

The covert narcissist is subtle and gentle in their approach. They try to evoke pity and are usually passive-aggressive. Dealing with this kind of narc means standing firm against their tactics, calling out their behavior, and reinforcing your boundaries.

The overt narcissist is more arrogant and visible. They like being the center of attention and can't stand humiliation. The best way to deal with them would be to starve them of any attention they may want from you and resist pandering to their ego.

The malignant narcissist is more violent and could be physically aggressive. They won't hesitate to lie, steal, and cheat. They may even be more prone to physical violence if goaded. The best approach is to limit contact with this kind of narcissist, show empathy if you have to engage, and leave as soon as possible.

Don't forget their common tactics

That one thing they always do that gets to you? Yeah. I'm sure you have a pretty good idea of what that is because we discussed it a lot.

For example, if their tactic is to call out your parenting or accuse you of being a bad parent, stand firm in your truth, repeat your affirmations to yourself, and do not budge. Instead, steer them back to the topic at hand.

If they often gaslight you and make you look silly, have your records or proof handy and calmly present them.

Keep a record of everything.

This is a great defense against gaslighting and helps you keep the upper hand. The best way to do this is to limit your communications to email alone or have a reliable third party around to witness your face-to-face communications. You can also record conversations if you can.

All these things will come in handy in the future.

Cut off their supply

Listen to me. This may be the most effective method of arming yourself against a narc. This means refusing to engage emotionally no matter what they say. Teach yourself to school your features, show no emotions, and keep things moving.

Did they just say they purposely had a vasectomy without telling you, even though they know you wanted more kids? Trust me, statements like that are deliberately crafted and delivered to make you lose control and to measure your reaction. It may be jarring, it may be difficult but do not react. Tell yourself. Do not react. That should be the mantra ringing in your mind as you face off with the narcissist.

Keep your distance

I cannot overemphasize how effective staying away from a toxic narc is. Let's throw away all former concepts of winning or losing. Staying away from them is not about hiding or being weak. It's a victory for you, a strategic step to weaken your foe. I'd compare it to cutting off the food supply to your enemy's camp. It's pure genius and a good strategy when you think about it.

If you're dealing with a malignant narcissist prone to fits of rage, it becomes doubly imperative that you stay away.

Remember always to keep your encounters short and simple. Don't be afraid to walk away at any point.

Stand Up for Yourself and Stop People-pleasing

One common question I get a lot is, "Was there something about me that attracted a narcissist to me?"

In a way, I feel conflicted about that question. I hate hearing it, but I appreciate it. Let me explain. I hate hearing it because it's usually a result of a self-blaming and self-hatred spiral. Most people ask this question to confirm what they've told themselves – that there's something wrong with them.

Even with the depth of information available to you about narcissism and why they do what they do, it's easy to still be dejected and blame yourself for attracting the wrong person into your life.

This is the point where I begin to appreciate the question. Because I have to explain that yes, there is a subcategory of people that narcissists are attracted to. These people are kind, warm, loving, and very empathetic. They are the kind of people to give their clothes off their backs to make someone else feel better

And how much more, the people they love?

But this isn't an indictment on those kinds of people. It doesn't mean they are weak or naive or deserve to be abused. No, it just means they are so good that even people who can't comprehend or appreciate them get attracted to them. And because narcs can be ruthless and deceptive, they'll deliberately set out to entice you by pretending to be exactly what you want. That's not your fault. It's all on them.

Unfortunately, being intimate with a narc can expose some unhealthy habits that you may have formed. We already dealt with one earlier – a lack of boundaries. The second unhealthy habit you probably have is people-pleasing.

Being a people-pleaser means that you're almost subconsciously driven to make everyone else happy, even if it means depriving yourself of the essentials.

You're a people pleaser if:

- You feel guilty telling people no.

- You crave other people's approval.

- You feel that doing things for others will make them like you.

- You have a hard time saying no.

- You're afraid that saying no means you're wicked, mean, or even selfish.

- You're constantly apologizing, even if you don't need to.

- You don't have any free time because you're always committing to doing things for other people.

- You think poorly of yourself.

Sounds familiar? Wanting to make other people happy may look good on paper, but in reality, it just makes you frustrated, angry, resentful, stressed, and anxious.

Here's how to stop being a people-pleaser:

Find your boundaries and decide what you want

Guess what? You have to decide what you want. And this extends to relationships outside the one with your ex. Do you like being spoken to sarcastically? Do you enjoy being teased about your weight? Do you like it when your children are rude to you?

No, I bet you really don't. So decide here and now to stop accepting it. It doesn't have to be a big declaration. Whenever you encounter someone leaving a bitter taste in your mouth, go back and reevaluate that situation. Find what you don't like and set a boundary around it. For example, you could decide to call out your sister the next time she talks about your weight in a derogatory manner. Or you could firmly tell your children to stop being rude and follow up with a punishment for their behavior. Start small.

You're free to keep reevaluating your boundaries and keep reworking them.

Take a few seconds

Next time, when someone asks you to do something you'd rather not do, instead of saying yes or painfully having to say no, ask for time to think about it and promise to get back to them. This saves you from saying no on the spot. You can weigh the request and see if you're really able to do it. If you can, and it's not something you will end up regretting, you can tell them yes later. If it's not, politely decline. If it's not a decision you can postpone, ask for a moment to think about it, and make your decision.

If you find out you can't do it, mentally prepare yourself to endure the process of saying no, then just say it.

Don't give excuses

The most important part of this whole process is refraining from giving excuses. Those just leave the door open to more questions and requests. Instead, say no without offering an explanation. It's hard, I know. But it's the best way. Be as firm and decisive as possible. No need for extras.

Be flexible

If you find yourself in the middle of doing something you'd rather not do, it's okay to still back out after explaining to whoever you're obligated to.

Or if, for example, you've committed to attending a party you don't really want to attend, you can compromise by leaving early instead of going for the whole thing.

Look, don't get lost here or overthink things. You need to stand up for yourself. And for your kids too. You need to stop being a people-pleaser. Just start, give yourself lots of grace and keep trying every day. You've got this.

Protecting Your Child Against the Narcissist's Tactics and Abuse

The thought of letting your child spend any time at all with an abusive or neglectful parent is scary. And make no mistake, you'd be hard-pressed to find a narcissist that's a fit parent to a child. Most of them consider children as yet another pawn to control, or they can see the child as your area of weakness, and trust me, they will not hesitate to exploit it. Remember that a narcissist has no empathy. So there are no limits to how far they may go.

Unfortunately, you may not be able to persuade the courts to give you sole custody of your child, and they have to keep interacting with the other parent. So once again, you have to pick up the slack and protect your child as much as you can.

Here's how to do it:

Be their solid rock

There's no telling how your narc ex will react during and after the divorce process. Their emotions and behaviors will likely oscillate. Your ex is also not above taking cheap shots at you in front of the children. Instead of thinking that they started it first and slinging words with them, be the calm parent. Be the one who never loses their cool. Be the one your kids can run to for a sense of stability.

It's not easy, I know. But you have to learn to control your anger, manage your emotions, and control your tongue, even when you're not in the same space with your ex. This helps them feel safe in the knowledge that you can handle anything, even the latest abusive thing your co-parent may have done.

Let them see you as a safe space where they can discuss anything without judgment. Teach them what abuse is if they are old enough to know and help them identify abusive behavior.

Don't contact them too much when they're with the other parent.

You need to reassure your child that you're reachable and that you're thinking of them. But apart from essential communications, limit your interaction with the child while they're with your co-parent. This effectively limits your contact with your ex and reduces the chances of triggering them when they hear your voice or note that you're frequently communicating.

Don't be emotional

Sometimes your ex may try to get a rise out of you simply to corroborate an earlier planted misconception in your child's mind that you're the bad/violent/aggressive parent.

Losing control in front of your child gives them the leeway to play the victim and make you look bad. And that can lead to a loyalty conflict, which is the last thing we want.

Validate your children's feelings

Sometimes (heck, most times!), the narcissist may devalue your child's feelings in one way or another. This is where your unconditional love, support, guidance, and empathy need to come into play. If you notice your child saying something demeaning about themselves or inferring that their other parent made them feel bad, correct that misconception without disparaging your ex. No matter what, that's still your kid's other parent, and they still love them.

Listen to them, rebuild their confidence, and teach them how to draw boundaries. For example, if they feel like your ex is saying something mean to them, you can tell them to excuse themselves to the restroom and recite some affirmations that you can teach them. Don't shy away from their attempts to express themselves, as painful as it may be for you to hear. Instead, acknowledge these feelings, hug them frequently, reassure them that you love, support, and believe them. Tell them that they can always come to you if they feel violated or abused in any way by your ex.

Help them calm down with the right words and reactions

If your child is old enough to understand the manipulative or wrong behaviors they have experienced, help them process their feelings the right way. While you shouldn't aim to deny the effects of their parent's behavior, try to be accommodating instead of going along to speak ill of your ex.

Disparaging your co-parent may make you feel better in the moment, but it does nothing positive for your child. The best thing to do is to agree that what your ex did wasn't right because the last thing you want to do is gaslight your kid and help them reframe their thoughts in a more positive direction.

For example, you could say, *"Yes, I know your mom said some hurtful things, but I hope you won't let that affect your peace today."*

Take action and get support

If your child reports an abusive incident, take them at their word and report to the appropriate quarters. If you need to get proof, try to get proof but prevent your child from coming in close contact with them again. They need to know that they can trust you to take their side any day, anytime.

If need be, encourage your child to speak to a therapist as well as your attorney. Don't hesitate to take steps as soon as you can.

The truth is, handling your kids and sharing them with an abusive co-parent can be tricky, and a one-size-fits-all approach may not be what you need. The bottom line remains that you need to ensure that your child feels loved and supported by you at all times, and you also need to stay watchful for other signs of abuse.

Chapter Six

Co-Parenting With The Narcissist Ex

"Narcissist parents do not know their children; they aren't interested in what they have to say unless it affects them."
— Tina Fuller

I remember speaking with Daryl, a friend of mine who had divorced his narcissist wife and managed to keep custody of the children. At first, he was happy that he had the kids to himself, and she never showed up for visitation whenever she was due. She claimed to be traveling from one part of the world to the other for business and was never available for weekends.

That was just fine by Darryl. He stopped reminding her about her visitation dates and focused on taking care of his girls. Then she began to drop by unannounced. Sometimes, she'd show up at school and take the girls out early to shop or the zoo. They began to look forward to spending time with her. So, of course, he couldn't object too much because it made the kids so happy. Louisa and Therese were ten years and seven years respectively, so they made her promise to come around more often. She would make the promise, and they would make elaborate plans for their next stint at her place, but she kept disappointing them. The worst part was that Darryl always had to break the news to them. He noticed that his girls were becoming increasingly sulky and withdrawn. They only brightened up whenever she called or when she came by.

When he spoke to his therapist, he realized that his ex-wife was emotionally neglecting the kids just to get back at him and that he needed to take a few steps and do some hard things to protect his girls.

When you're dealing with a narcissist, it pays off always to be watchful. If it seems like they're being compliant and quiet, you can bet they're up to something. If they're giving trouble and making your life hellish, that's about their usual modus operandi.

The really sad part is that it may take you a while to figure out what they're up to, and just like Darryl, you may find out that they have no qualms about hurting the children just to get to you. Unfortunately.

We're going to see how we can handle these challenges and what we can do if co-parenting doesn't work. Just like Darryl, you will need to do some hard things that we'll look at in this chapter, but I promise you that it's all worth it.

Co-parenting With a Narcissist is Challenging

I once heard someone I suspected to be a narcissist talk about his family. You could tell he was really proud of his three children, and even though they were just in high school, he already knew what he wanted each child to study in college. He couldn't stop going on about how brilliant, adventurous, and perfect his children were.

The part that stuck out for me was how he never once mentioned their mother or her efforts to raise the children. To hear him tell it, you would not be wrong to assume that the children were raised only by him. Imagine my surprise when the rest of his family came in, and their mother accompanied them. My suspicions about his narcissistic tendencies were confirmed when I noticed that he gave his eldest son preferential treatment and didn't pay as much attention to the others. Oh, you can also bet that he was subtly putting down his wife at the dinner table while sounding relaxed and jovial.

This is a frequent tactic used by narcissistic parents with multiple kids. They often select one child as their favorite and may neglect or criticize the others excessively. They do this to better manipulate their children, and unfortunately, the favorite child may also become a narcissist.

This is one of the many challenges that may arise when co-parenting with a narc. Some other common challenges you may face are:

They will go ahead to ignore all your ground rules and break as many boundaries as possible.

What do you do when your ex starts to change the rules of parenting you already set or maybe even both agreed on in the beginning? For example, they know that you've set bedtime for 8 pm for the children, but they let them stay up till 12. They know that you don't allow sweets before meals, but they still let your kids have as many scoops of ice cream as they want. The scariest part comes when you realize they're pulling all these stunts just to get back at you.

They'll ignore court rules and agreements.

What will the narcissist not do to make your life miserable? Pretty much nothing. They do not mind going as low as they can or being as petty as possible, just to frustrate you. Does the court say they have visitation rights every 4th weekend of the month? Watch them turn up without warning on the second weekend in the month, with a lame excuse for not being available at the appointed time and take the kids. They may keep them for longer than the weekend without advance warning. They'll lord the fact that they pay for child support over you.

They'll badmouth you to the kids behind your back

I think this one is a given. Your narc ex has no restrictions or obligations to respect you. They'll talk bad about you and lie about you to the children behind your back. They'll criticize you openly in front of your kids, and they won't consider your feelings or even the kid's feelings.

They won't play nice, even for the children's sake

This seems like I'm just reiterating everything we've talked about so far, but it's true! Are you counting on them to support you in one way or another because of the children? Yeah, no, they won't. The fact is that they can't love your children the same way you do. They simply do not have enough empathy to achieve this. The sooner you realize that the better for all of us.

These are by no means all the obstacles you may face when co-parenting with a narc. Look, I get it; it's hard. It's difficult, and sometimes, it's downright impossible. So what do you do in those cases? You give up on co-parenting and move on to something else. More on this later.

What to Expect When Co-parenting

Co-parenting with a non-narcissist spouse requires a lot of communication, cooperation, and understanding. In this scenario, both parents are focused on their child's emotional, financial, mental, and physical needs. Both parents are willing to come to several compromises just to get the best for their kids.

Not so the narcissist parent. They focus more on their own emotional wants and desires than the child. That means that getting back at you may be their desire at that moment, and they'll go after it the best way they can. They definitely won't stop to think about the kids or how their actions may affect them.

That's what it means to co-parent with a narc in a nutshell. You may expect the narcissist parent to exhibit abusive behaviors toward the children. They may be emotionally affected by the actions of a narcissist parent, but yet they'll keep loving them and showing them affection because that's what children do.

It's possible that your narcissist ex may emotionally manipulate your child. They may see the child as an extension of you and take out their frustrations on the children. If your child is independent or outspoken, the narcissist will not hesitate to break them down bit by bit just to gain control of that child.

Your ex may also lie against your children to put you against them. While it's possible for children to take advantage of the split to turn their parents against each other or to trick them into getting their way, don't be quick to accuse your child solely on your ex's word. Sit them down and calmly ask them without sounding accusatory. Try to prevent the situation from escalating as much as possible by limiting contact or setting out sterner rules. Help your child understand what you're trying to achieve.

Narcissist parents may bully and try to control their children especially when they're visiting. Make sure that your child feels safe enough to talk to you and take swift action if they report any such incident to you.

I think we can admit here that co-parenting with a narc may be particularly impossible most of the time. If your ex is the sort that's making things difficult for you, don't feel bad or like you've failed. Simply switch from co-parenting to parallel parenting.

Parental Alienation is a Thing

We've talked a bit about loyalty conflicts in the previous chapter and another thing we have to discuss as an extension of this is parental alienation.

So what is it? It's what happens when one parent takes deliberate, planned steps to isolate their child from the other parent by portraying the other parent as bad through their words and conduct. The endgame is to create suspicion and hostility toward the other parent in the child's mind.

Does that sound familiar? This is more common than you may expect and is frequently done by narcissists. Parental alienation is usually a subtle, subconscious programming done on the child by the parent. For example, if your partner is fond of telling your kids that you don't love them or want a new set of children instead of them. Those are pretty mild accusations. Pretty severe accusations would be if your partner lied to your kids that you hit them even though you never did, or they claimed that you're a wicked person who's trying to separate the kids from the other parent.

Even if the accusations are mild, they can be very damaging if they're repeated frequently and the children start to believe them. Eventually, the child may not want to see the other parent because they truly believe what they've been told.

How can you tell if your child is being programmed or brainwashed into hating you? This can also serve as a guideline to check if you're alienating your child from the other parent as well.

Some important signs are:

Your child suddenly hates you and never wants to spend time with you

If your child starts criticizing you or finding faults with anything you do, especially if they previously were not like that, it could be a sign that your ex may be alienating you from your child. Some notable things to look out for is the fact that your child may start using strange adult vocabulary or mannerisms that they may not have used before.

Another telltale sign is that your child doesn't feel bad or guilty about hating you. They show no remorse about it and do not mind telling others about it. In fact, sometimes, your child may not openly tell you that they don't like you (duh), so they can tell their friends or other people they're close to instead. If they totally dislike you without giving room for your positive attributes, that could be another pointer to an alienation situation.

Your child also doesn't like your family members or people associated with you

If your child also extends that hatred or dislike to your family members like your siblings, cousins, or parents, it's a clear sign that they are being brainwashed into wanting to leave you.

It's especially obvious when your child previously loved your siblings or parents. Something fishy may be going on there.

Your child has total support for the other parent

It's not strange for children to think that their parents hung the moon, especially when they're much younger. However, if your child is a bit older, and they suddenly seem to support your ex a hundred percent, especially if they were not like that before, you might want to look closely into that.

Your child can't give a coherent reason for criticizing you.

If your child is asked why they're so disapproving of you, they may not be able to give strong evidence or concrete justifications to back why they feel that way about you.

Or they may give a reason that's not true or completely true. For example, they may say they don't like you anymore because you sent them up to bed while their show was on. Yes, you did send them away from the TV, but you do that every day. So what's so special about this particular occasion?

These signs are especially valid if the child had a very strong relationship with the parent that they suddenly do not like as well as an equally solid relationship with the co-parent.

Let's look at things as truthfully as possible; you could be guilty of alienating your child from your ex, especially if they are toxic and you feel that your child is better off without them anyway. I mean, sometimes you don't even have to make up stories about your co-parent; all you have to do is tell the pure, unvarnished truth and stop shielding your child. Well, guess what? Telling your child too many details about your ex is also a form of parental alienation. You're bringing your child into an issue that should remain between you and your ex. You can bet they'd get angry and start judging the other person.

Another way you might be alienating your child from the parent is by preventing your child from seeing the parent while lying to the child that your ex doesn't want to see them. This perpetuates the idea that your co-parent doesn't care about the child and will naturally make the child sad and eventually dislike the other parent.

Parental alienation may also look like undermining the other parent's authority and making them look like a bad parent. For example, if you know that your co-parent wants your child to wear their shin guards when riding but you tell your kid that the other parent is being excessive and doesn't know what they're talking about and you encourage them to ride without any form of protection, you've undermined the other parent's authority. You've made it look like it's okay for your child to disregard whatever the other person says and made them a less effective parent. As time goes on, the child will start to doubt that the other parent is really acting in their best interest and may start to slowly dislike them.

Unfortunately, alienation has a lot of negative effects on your kid and has been officially classified as emotional child abuse (NCSC). Children who experience parental alienation often:

- Have no empathy.

- Learn that it's okay to see others as competition with the 'us vs them' mentality that parental alienation fosters.

- Feel neglected or are actually neglected in the process.

- Learn to lie to others and may twist the reality of situations to suit their narrative.

- Feel a loss of self-respect.

- Feel a lot of guilt and anxiety later on because they feel like they ruined their relationship with the parent.

- Have academic problems.

If you suspect some alienation is happening, you need to speak to a therapist to help reunite the child with the alienated parent. If necessary, you may need to speak to your lawyer and start formal court proceedings to put a stop to it. Even though this may be unnecessarily traumatic for your child, it may be necessary.

How Parents Cause Loyalty Conflict

Loyalty conflicts happen all the time. We know they happen when a child feels compelled to choose sides or pick between two parents they love. This is a very uncomfortable feeling for any child to experience, and it places them under a lot of mental stress.

Experiencing the divorce may be traumatic for the child in the first place; if they're placed in a position where they feel they have to choose between both of their parents, they will definitely be distressed at the thought.

A child who is experiencing a loyalty conflict may throw tantrums, have headaches, or cry whenever they have to go to the other parent. It's usually no cause for alarm because they tend to feel better shortly after they get to the other parent's place. They may also act differently around each parent and be unexcited about seeing the other parent. For the most part, parents are guilty of causing loyalty conflicts. Arguing in the presence of their children is a good way to cause loyalty conflicts. Spilling details and facts that should not be said in front of your child while arguing can lead to the kid judging both parents based on their behavior and picking a side. Badmouthing your ex or subtly expressing distrust or animosity towards them can also make your child feel compelled to take a side. It may be hard, but control is necessary and will pay off in the future.

What about step-parents or people you'd like to date? That's another factor to consider. Your child may see your or your ex's new partner as an interloper and may view that relationship as a betrayal of the original family unit. It's best to help your child see the new partner as just one more adult who cares for them. If your ex has a new partner, be cordial and polite whenever you see them, and try not to make your child feel like you don't like the new partner.

Loyalty conflicts need to be noted and managed as soon as possible so that your child can get the best out of the divorce.

When To Choose Parallel Parenting Instead

We've mentioned parallel parenting a couple of times in this chapter, and we'll take a better look at it now.

We're all familiar with the concept of co-parenting, and it's been lauded as the perfect solution to raise your kids when there's been a divorce. Co-parenting involves both parents working together to raise their children, and the aim is to provide a stable environment that supports the kids and helps them adjust well to their new reality.

It means coming together to plan the day-to-day details of child care, making decisions that concern the children together, and frequently communicating with each other.

Here's something you may need to hear: co-parenting may be impossible for you if your ex is a narcissist. I'm spelling it out clearly because I've had some people feel guilty for not being able to successfully co-parent with their narc ex. As you might imagine, they kept putting up with their tactics and trying to make peace over and over again 'for the kids'. Needless to say it wasn't very successful at all and led to more stress than good.

So please don't feel bad about not co-parenting. Don't feel like you've failed or that you have to keep trying for the kids. The best thing is to make peace with this fact right off the bat and keep it moving.

Parallel parenting is a much more realistic solution to sharing custody with a narc ex. It's a hands-off approach to parenting your kids. No one needs to collaborate or agree to a particular way of parenting; each parent does whatever they think is best for the child and doesn't interfere with what the other parent does.

It's great because it reduces the chances of conflict and limits contact between parents. It also helps you reinforce all those nice boundaries we talked about earlier. Children who experience parallel parenting also have some form of stability because they know what to expect from each parent.

Here's the truth, co-parenting isn't necessarily better than parallel parenting. It all depends on what works for your family. Don't fall into the comparison trap, feel inadequate, or worry that your kids will suffer simply because you're practicing parallel parenting. Remember that every family is different, and you're simply trying to meet your family's unique needs.

I know we've said that this method is best for high-conflict scenarios because we're trying to prevent your kids from getting exposed to the conflict. But, this method cannot hold if your child is being abused one way or another by your ex. If that is the case, limit contact with the abusive partner and file for full custody on the advice of your attorney, of course.

Part Three

Moving On With Grace

Take a deep breath and realize that you made it through! Learning about your narcissist ex, reliving those not-so-great memories, taking the bold step to do some self-reflection and forgive yourself, choosing to put yourself and your kids first, and accepting that your toxic ex will never change can't have been easy. Yet you've done it.

Now, let's focus more on you and the kids. Is it possible to co-parent positively? What is positive co-parenting? At this point, you may be dealing with surly, uncooperative children, or maybe they even blame you for the split. You know that your relationship with your child has changed for the worse, and you need to know how to fix it. Can you really improve your relationship with your child? The good news is, yes, you absolutely can. We'll look at ways to make your child bond better with you and to help them rely on you more through this process. We'll help them become resilient and able to handle whatever challenges they may face as they go along.

Then we'll take a closer look at you. Is it really possible to move on and have a better life? Can you love again? What if you end up with another narcissist? We'll see that it is indeed possible to live, laugh, and love again. Instead of burying yourself in taking care of the kids or ignoring your needs, we'll see how you can give yourself a break and take care of yourself. Living with a narcissist most likely has given you a false self-image and self-belief; we'll see how to move away from that into a mental space where you love yourself, appreciate yourself, and want the best for yourself.

You may even be open to looking for love. But how can anyone love you if you can't love yourself? The best way to teach someone to love you is to love yourself first. Not necessarily romantic love but your friendships, relationships with your family members, and other significant connections are to be considered.

We'll also see how you can carry your kids along, so it doesn't feel like you're abandoning them.

This part is all about you living your best life despite everything that's happened. Someone out there is going to be inspired by your story and your journey, so don't hold back!

Chapter Seven

Positive Co-Parenting: How To

"Behind every young child who believes in himself is a parent who believed first"
— Matthew Jacobson

Parenting is a lifelong task. It's fun, scary, and exhilarating. It's like walking a tightrope between two skyscrapers 400m high. No, scratch that. Parenting is like walking a tightrope 400m above the ground while juggling apples that seem to increase in number every time you toss one into the air.

It's having to deal with curious kids, being a good example to your children, fearing that you're making a mistake with raising them, or wondering if you could do better with them. It's about feeling a little sad when your kid doesn't want to spend as much time with you anymore. It's wanting to keep them sheltered forever but realizing they need to find their feet in the world. It's the awareness that one mistake, especially in the aftermath of a divorce, could alter how they regard life and fundamentally change them forever.

It's a whole lot, but we'll get through it together. Is there a style of parenting that helps you meet your kids' emotional needs while encouraging them and solving their problems? Is there a style of parenting that moves away from shaming, hostility, name calling, and focusing on negative emotions? Can you enjoy parenting your kids without passing on whatever trauma you inherited?

Yes. That's the short answer. The long answer is the next section.

Well, go on, don't wait on my account.

The Concept of Positive Parenting

I particularly like the way positive parenting was described as an ongoing relationship between parents and children that includes teaching, caring, communicating, leading, and providing for the needs of the children in a consistent and unconditional manner (Seay, 2014).

Positive parenting focuses on being empowering while being nurturing. It involves setting boundaries that help your child develop to the fullest. It's about being non-violent, affectionate, sensitive to your child's needs and emotions, providing emotional security, and rewarding accomplishments while supporting your child's best interests.

The point here is to teach your child to be disciplined so they aren't left with shattered self-esteem. It's not a permissive relationship or a practice where the child becomes selfish, greedy, spoiled, and uncaring. None of that. It's a two-way relationship where the child is taught to respect the parents, and the parents also respect their child. It's about teaching your child all the good things they need to learn without breaking their spirit or leaving them with complexes that may take years and several thousands of dollars in therapy to solve. It's the fine balance between being warm, loving, and considerate without being permissive.

A lot of people have the wrong idea about this style of parenting. Some think it's about being that parent that doesn't spank their child. Others have said it's about never saying 'No' to their kids. Some have denounced it as a parenting style that raises children who don't know how to react to negative emotions or situations because their parents have shielded them. Truthfully, if it's not practiced intentionally and carefully, it can go wrong, and all your worst fears may be realized.

You may have been exposed to a parenting style that is harsher and less supportive. Sure, you turned out fine, for the most part, but shouldn't your kids have a better experience than you did? One mistake I see many parents make is wildly overcompensating for their own parents' deficiencies with their kids.

For example, Christine's parents were both doctors who were very disciplined and well-celebrated. They had three kids, and all three children were expected to go to medical school and become doctors, just like their parents. Naturally, she rebelled against them and decided to become an artist, to her parents' shame and horror.

Her other siblings were doctors, so her parents paid a lot more attention to them, and she was left feeling like crap. She swore she'd never force her own children to do something they didn't want or judge them for their choices.

This is a noble aspiration, but we have to realize that Christine may make many mistakes along the line simply because she's trying to prevent repeating what happened with her parents with her child. She may not want to speak up if she realizes that her kid is failing science-based subjects in high school. She may decide to let her child go to community college instead of a bigger college (which she can afford) simply because the child wants to be with their friend or significant other. She may choose to turn a blind eye if she catches her child smoking pot just because she doesn't want to influence their life choices in any way.

See how that's a recipe for disaster?

On the other hand, if Christine had realized that positive parenting was best for her child, she would try to find out why her kid was failing. She would try to empathize with them, identify their emotions, and try her best to support them. All this can be accomplished while letting the kid know that they have to focus more and study so they can start passing their subjects again. She would acknowledge her child's reluctance to be separated from their friend or significant other in college but help them understand there are ways to maintain contact while each person is working to achieve their separate goals. She would gently but firmly dissuade her child from smoking pot by trying to understand why they're doing it in the first place, explaining why it's harmful, and asking them to stop.

In a nutshell, positive parenting is about focusing on the issue at hand alongside your child, supporting your child the best way you can while solving their issues, and reinforcing your relationship and connection with your kid but not ignoring their wrongdoings. It's about ensuring that your kids experience the consequences of their actions as laid down by you but still helping them understand that their relationship with you will always be safeguarded.

It's about being consistent, creating a nurturing environment, helping your child develop by supporting them emotionally, and raising a fully functioning adult at the end of the day.

We'll look at more practical examples of positive parenting and its benefits, in a bit.

Improving Your Relationship With Your Child

Adam was really frustrated because he could feel that his child wasn't interested in a relationship with him anymore. His son would rather spend more time at the neighbor's place than hang out with him. They no longer had the long conversations he used to enjoy.

He knew that this could happen, especially as Adam Jr became a teenager, and of course, he knew that divorce was hard on his 14-year-old son. Adam felt like he'd made a big mess of things and didn't want to be a stranger to his only child. He had tried getting his son presents, taking them out to a game, and even sitting him down for a talk. But all his efforts ended with a blank stare and an expression of disinterest.

He didn't know where to start or what to do. You may not be in Adam's exact same shoes, but you've probably noticed that your relationship with your kid needs a lot of work. Maybe you're tired of being frequently told to *"Get out of my room mom/dad!"* or you're constantly served with a special "I hate you, you've ruined my life!" now that the divorce is done.

You may want to pretend to be unbothered or feel like your child will come around eventually. That's a dangerous assumption because what if they never reconnect with you? What if you end up estranged from your kid in the future?

Thankfully, some steps can be taken to make your relationship with your child better. Another point of gratitude may be that these steps don't require setting up a fancy, expensive vacation or buying the most expensive item on their wish list. In fact, some of these steps are things you can do right now or before they go to bed.

An important disclaimer here is that these steps require consistency, focus, and a pure intention to bond better with your kid. One thing that's for sure is that children can and will spot any traces of dishonesty from a mile away. This is why you need to actually want to connect with them more and be willing to do what it takes.

Ready? Let's get into it. Some practical steps to improving your relationship with your child (no matter how old they may be) are:

Listen to them

I'm sure you enjoy feeling like you're being heard whenever you speak. As a parent, you may not have realized that you've fallen into the habit of listening to react or to lay down laws instead of listening to really understand. This gets harder when your child has done something to offend or disappoint you. But instead of jumping the gun and reacting harshly or trying to make them see how they've disappointed you, why not slow down to listen to what they have to say? Your kids want to feel heard and validated too. Let them state their opinions and possibly their reasons for their actions. Even if you don't agree with them or you're really angry, take a breather and find a solution that considers their feelings and opinions.

Be deliberate about spending time with them

To be very specific, I'm talking about quality time here. This means a time with little to no interactions and freedom of expression. If you have more than one child, it's best to spend time alone with each of them so that they can feel loved and special. This time could be when you're dropping them off at practice or school, or maybe when you're eating dinner together at the table or even hanging out on the couch after a meal.

If you don't know how to start or you suspect your kid may feel awkward about it, spend this time doing something you both love. It could be fishing, going shopping, or shooting hoops at the back. Make sure you put your phone away during this period and gently ask them questions or bring up a comfortable topic. You can encourage them to share a confidence with you by telling them something private (but not too weighty) about you. Promise them that their secrets are safe with you (and mean it too). This will show them that you're a priority to them and help them trust you more as time goes on.

Acknowledge their feelings

Simply pausing to validate your child's feelings will go a long way to make them feel understood. It doesn't have to be anything fancy; you can simply say something like, *"I understand that you're hurt because XYZ and I can relate with that. I would be very unhappy if I were in your shoes too. But …"*

This singular act of validating their feelings will help your child see you as an ally instead of the opposition. Keep encouraging them to express their emotions by asking *" How do you feel about that?"* If they say they're hurt, angry or upset, don't brush over their feelings and rush to make your point. This tip is gold, and it's something you can start practicing today.

Set your boundaries and respect theirs

No matter how much you love your kid and want the best for them, boundaries are necessary to foster a healthy relationship for you both. Establish reasonable boundaries like 'No phones at the dinner table' or ' No yelling during discussions'. Keeping to them may seem like you're being mean to your child, but it's a way to help them grow. If they disregard your boundaries, attach appropriate consequences and discuss with them when you're dishing out these consequences.

In the same way, you need to respect your child's boundaries. As they get older, they become more independent and want to set their own boundaries. It's your job to guide them in the setting of appropriate boundaries as well as to respect said boundaries. For example, if they ask you to knock before entering their room, try to do so. Doing this will also teach them to respect your own boundaries as well.

Tell them you love them

This may sound like a no-brainer, but it's very important. Being verbally affectionate with your child helps them feel comfortable with expressing their own emotions. Apart from telling them, you should also show them that you love them and you care. Hug them, send them texts talking about how you love them, buy them a little gift or surprise them with something you know they like. Try to make them laugh, laugh at yourself with them and play with them.

They may roll their eyes, ignore you or try to avoid you, but I promise, it works! Keep at it, and you'll be amazed!

Strategies For Positive Co-Parenting

Let's move on a bit and talk about positive co-parenting. How can you implement it with your kids? When you take a positive approach to co-parenting, you're giving your kids a boost in their self-growth and positive development. You're helping them improve their social skills as well as their problem-solving skills. You're teaching your kids to be more creative, expressive, and self-determined. You're helping them learn accountability and responsibility. Of course, by default, their self-esteem and self-confidence goes up a notch or ten.

You may be wondering what the best age for practicing positive co-parenting is. Don't worry; you've not missed the bus. The fact is, you can start practicing positive co-parenting at any time and still reap its rewards. That being said, you can start with babies under the age of one.

You may want to know if there's a particular age where even positive parenting doesn't seem to work. Why, you curious Kate, there just may be an answer to the question!

Interestingly, a study done in 2015 has found that the tween years in children may just be the most difficult years to parent your child. This means that middle school children may be the most emotionally exhausting and unrewarding age range to experience. The study found that mothers of teens were more likely to be depressed than mothers of babies and toddlers (Luthar,2016). Of course, raising a baby or toddler can be physically exhausting but also emotionally rewarding because babies are naturally affectionate. Observing all their developmental milestones, like walking, helps boost our sense of pride and accomplishment.

Cue the rudeness, defiance, selfishness, and backtalk. So yeah, add that on top of a divorce, and it could be hard. But positive co-parenting becomes invaluable in this kind of setup because the principles involved will still help your teen (or tween) get past this. A huge source of consolation during this phase is that it doesn't last forever. But this doesn't mean you shouldn't pay close attention to your kids or try to help them through.

Right. Now that we've established that this parenting style is the bomb, how can you start practicing it? Let's look at some effective strategies you could start using immediately!

1) Put your child's needs first

Your child is the focus and the sole beneficiary of this whole concept. It's only natural that you put them first. This may sound like we're flogging a dead horse here, but it's important enough to warrant a second, third, and fifteenth mention. Trying to co-parent with a narc will, more often than not, be a very messy and exhausting experience. It may be a constant battle where your ex is trying to get back at you by being as uncooperative as possible. I bet you're wondering how you can trust them to put the children first. Well, you can't. The burden of making sure that your kids are fine will have to rest on your shoulders.

Putting them first will mean considering them before you make a decision. For example, your co-parent should have brought the kids back from the weekend at their place, but they didn't. Instead, they took the kids for a trip to the park with their new partner without informing you ahead of time. After a few frantic phone calls to your ex, who deliberately did not answer the first two times, you discover that your kids have already been promised to extend their weekend by two more days and that they have met the new boyfriend/girlfriend without your consent or awareness. Oh, and you didn't even know there was a new partner in the picture, and you've not even prepared them for that possibility. How would you react? I expect you'd want to go over there, take the kids, and maybe scream bloody murder. Perfectly understandable.

But because you're thinking of the kids, and you don't want to ruin their fun or let them hear you arguing with the other parent, plus they don't have school anyway, you decide to let it slide and simply record it with proof. Instead of calling them, you decide to send a well-thought-out email that's professional and polite. That doesn't sound nearly as satisfying as cussing them out, but it's better for the kids. See what I mean?

2) Don't try to micromanage your co-parent

Try not to stress about the small stuff. You're more likely to get frustrated by your narc ex if you choose to fight about everything. Little decisions like meal choices, bedtimes, and outings can be brushed over. But the big ones like medical care, choice of school, and similar things should be agreed on, preferably, in a legal document. If one parent flouts this arrangement, then legal action can be taken after an attempt to discuss them has been made.

3) Be positive about your co-parent

Hold on! Before you leave in outrage, hear me out first. Yes, I know it takes a lot not to badmouth your ex in front of your kid, even though they deserve it. A lot of self-discipline and restraint. I know. Taking a further step to be positive about your co-parent around your kid may even be harder, but it's worth it. Acknowledging your co-partner's positive side shows that you still value and appreciate them, which encourages your kid to express their positive opinions about them without feeling guilty. It also helps you feel better. Saying something like "Your dad sure knows how to play basketball well, doesn't he?" is a great way to express positivity.

4) Be cautious with introducing new partners

Of course, you'd want to form new relationships and get closer to other people. Even though you may feel that your new partner is 'the one', it's best to wait until the relationship has a great degree of permanence before you introduce them to your child.

Also, don't involve the new partner in decision-making when it concerns your child. Do not let them interact with your ex when it comes to issues affecting your child. This averts the likelihood of conflict and prevents the unnecessary drama that may accompany it.

To recap, doing what's best for your child, acknowledging your ex's right to have a say in parenting your child, working together to agree on some basic rules for raising the child, letting go of negative feelings like anger and resentment while concentrating on being warm and loving are the basics of being a positive co-parent.

If you cannot successfully co-parent with your narcissist ex, parallel parenting works just as well. The great part is that you can apply these same principles of positive parenting to it.

Why Positive Co-Parenting Is Important

Once in a while, I get people who tell me stuff like, *"Y'all are getting distracted by fancy terms and titles. I'll raise my kid to respect me and to know their place. I'll raise them not to be lazy or spoiled, and they'll learn not to disobey me. That's my style of positive parenting, and it works for me."*

I mean, no arguments here. Everyone is free to raise their kids as they see fit, so I'm not going to tell you what to do. Instead, let's look at what research has to say about positive parenting and its benefits, shall we?

When we get down to the nitty-gritty of things, we'll see that adopting the positive parenting style helps to teach children what to do and why they should do it. This is best so they can replicate these behaviors when no one is looking and also without a need for a reward. The major components seen in positive parenting are:

Parents actively listen to their children to understand what they're thinking.

This helps the parents identify logical fallacies or misunderstandings and correct them before they fester.

Parents help their children understand structure and stability by setting boundaries, laying down rules, and attaching consequences.

This should be consistently maintained so the child can predict how their parents will react if they perform a particular action. Inevitably, the children test the boundaries and break the rules. Instead of merely ensuring the previously discussed consequences are enacted, this moment is used as a teachable moment.

The child learns how to restrain themselves from repeating that action, understands why what they did was wrong, gets reassured that their parents love them even though they are enforcing the consequences, and learns the restraint needed to stop breaking that particular rule. The end result is that the child understands and identifies with the discipline given out and doesn't just obey orders out of fear of punishment but rather from a logical understanding of the offense.

Parents dwell on the positive aspects of the child's behavior as well as emphasizing positive emotions and opinions.

This means taking the time to play with them, making them laugh, and commending their good behavior. A good tip to note here is that it's better to emphasize how that good deed made them feel instead of focusing on how it made you feel.

For example, you can say " *Wow, you must be so proud of yourself for finishing those vegetables, just like you promised Mommy you would.*" Instead of saying, " *Wow, I'm so proud of you for finishing your vegetables.*" This teaches them to look for validation and praise internally instead of waiting for external validation. This will also teach them to carry out positive behaviors when no one else is looking.

Parents admit that they're not perfect.

Another often overlooked part is that it's okay to admit that parenting can be stressful despite your positive approach. Sometimes, it's okay just to sit down and accept that there are some things you can't control. It's entirely normal to tell yourself that you're doing your best, and that's alright too. You're a human, after all, and your needs deserve to be met as well.

These components are very important, and they also help guide the administration of discipline whenever it's needed. To be a positive parent, sometimes, you need to begin with the end in mind. Ask yourself, what kind of person would you like your child to be in the future? If they were a full-grown adult, would you yell at them or attempt to spank them? Very unlikely; you'd rather gently discuss with them like a rational adult.

Now, I'm not by any means asking you to treat your 7-year-old like a 25-year-old. No, this exercise is for you. It's to help you learn to extend respect and empathy to your child whenever you speak to them. Of course, it applies to children of all ages, and its benefits can be seen in different children's age ranges.

Positive parenting has been found to help children adapt to their school environment better and be better motivated. Toddlers and infants are also not left out. This study found that infants were increasingly motivated (Joussemet, 2008). Younger children were found to have healthier parent-child attachments and remarkable cognitive and social development (Juffer,2008). Another study found that it increased self-esteem among adolescents (Duineveld, 2017).

For adolescents, problem behaviors like yelling, bullying, and truancy were noted to be reduced while their self-esteem, educational aspirations, career aspirations, and mental resilience skyrocketed after being exposed to positive parenting strategies (Sandler, 2015). Another interesting analysis found that positive parenting reduced family conflict and stress, reduced problem behaviors in children, improved the family connection, and made both parents and children more resilient (Kumpfer,1998).

All in all, there are numerous benefits to be gained by practicing positive parenting. It's not a one-size-fits-all approach; it considers your unique circumstances. Once the principles behind it are adhered to, you can expect to see a significant improvement in your parenting experience.

Helping Your Kids Develop Mental Resilience

What comes to mind when you hear the word resilience? I used to liken it to a famous mountain not far from my favorite getaway spot in the woods. But now I realize that perhaps it's more accurately likened to a river. Not a lake, not a stream, but a river.

If I had to define 'Resilience' in less than five words, I'd say it's 'the ability to adapt'. Being mentally resilient is the ability to work through challenging situations and cope with stress. It's being able to recover from failure, trauma, or any other kind of challenge. It's about putting oneself back together after falling apart. It's like flowing on and finding a way to either penetrate any obstacles or work around them.

You'll agree that it's an essential life skill because life is generally not a bed of roses. It's especially important for kids because studies have shown that children who are mentally resilient are mentally strong and can reach their full potential thanks to their courage and confidence (Masten, 2018).

Mentally resilient children are often willing to take healthy risks because they're not afraid to fail. They have a strong sense of curiosity, are brave, and often trust their instincts. They are also more likely to push themselves out of their comfort zone.

Thankfully, mental resilience is a skill that can be taught. It's important to raise mentally resilient kids because, as a parent, you can't protect them from everything, and you shouldn't. They need to learn how to look out for themselves when you're not there.

How can you help your children become mentally resilient? The basic principles are to:

1) Show them how to process and control their emotions.

2) Teach them how and when to take positive action.

3) Help them learn to foster a positive and optimistic outlook on life and themselves as well.

These tips are a great place to start:

Don't be a helicopter parent

As a parent, your natural urge is to help your kid whenever they're stuck. At best, you'd want to teach them how to achieve what they need. At worst, you'll take over the problem by yourself and deny them the opportunity to solve it on their own.

If you want mentally resilient kids, you'll need to learn to be patient and ask questions instead of giving lectures. Ask leading questions guaranteed to help them arrive at the answer by themselves.

Teach them how to modulate their emotions

Another big mistake many parents make is teaching their children to mask their emotions. To prevent them from being sad or annoyed, you'll find the average parent trying to cheer up a sad child or encouraging their child to repress their anger.

To teach them mental resilience, you're better off allowing them to understand and process their emotions. This helps them to get familiar with said emotions because they'll be experiencing them a lot in the future, and they also learn how to handle the feelings. In the future, this will make them more equipped to handle challenges.

Allow them to make mistakes

Mistakes are naught but an opportunity to learn. Preventing your child from making mistakes will insulate them from the feelings accompanying them and leave them wholly unprepared to face those mistakes in the future.

Teach them that mistakes are part of life and a great way to learn. Help them to understand that feeling ashamed or embarrassed isn't necessary. Teach them how to avoid that mistake the next time instead.

Let your child take risks

If your child says they want to perform in a school play or try out a sport but you know that they're painfully shy or aren't athletic, what will you do? Should you talk them out of it or allow them to proceed?

I say let them proceed. Allowing them to take healthy risks, like the examples I gave, will teach them that it's OK to go out of their comfort zone. When they take these risks, they learn to push themselves.

Teach them how to reframe negative thoughts

Teaching your child a realistic view of things without losing their sense of optimism is a valuable lesson. Kids can't be mentally resilient if the opposition comes from their own minds. Help them cancel negative thoughts and replace them with positive thoughts. Teach them how to recite positive affirmations that address any area of weakness.

There are a lot of methods to teach mental resilience to your kids, but this is a perfect place to start.

Chapter Eight

Rebuilding Your Life

"It's never too late—never too late to start over, never too late to be happy."
—Jane Fonda

Life as you know it has changed. It's important to accept that fact for what it is and internalize it. Things will not be the same. Trying to get things back to what they were is like a hamster running on a wheel, unproductive and stressful.

I'm saying this because you may not realize it, but it's possible that a tiny part of you still holds on to the past. A small fragment of your consciousness still wishes to recapture some elements of the past. Maybe the days when you were still in love with your ex or those times when you seemed like a real family. Or maybe it's remembering when your children were young, cuddly and adorable, not disdainful and prickly like they are now. Heck, you may even wish for those days when your body was better and you were younger and had more energy.

Well, guess what? The past is the past. Dwelling on it instead of moving on won't yield anything. I want you to really and truly commit to moving on. To understand that you can let go of the past entirely.

It may seem daunting but don't worry. I'll help you.

Take Your Time: Don't Rush Things

I know I talked about how you need to move on and let go of the past. That's still valid, and the most important part of that process is letting yourself heal properly. This means you shouldn't force your grieving process and rush through it, ignoring the work you need to do. This also means that you're absolutely not allowed to cling to that grieving phase for too long.

It's easy to put your head down and focus on caring for the children. Heck, you'll most likely get distracted from the serious work of self-healing by the antics your narc ex is sure to play. Or maybe you've even given up entirely, and you've decided to live a life where you're effectively numb to your personal life and only come alive when the kids are involved. No matter where you are right now, you need to know that other people have walked that path, and they've come out of the experience a better version of themselves.

While I know that you have to give yourself time and space to work through everything that's happened properly, I need you to fix your mind on the person you'd like to be in the future. You know that version of yourself that you think you can't achieve? That vision that's so scary that you'd rather not think about it? Yeah. I'd like you to boldly explore it without trying to think of the details; just explore your best future self and get comfortable with them. Fix that image in your mind even as you work through this process.

When the time to move on comes, your future self will beckon you to start the journey. Oh, did I say beckon? More like push you. Good luck!

Self-care is Important

What does self-care look like for a person who's divorced? How does the split affect your decision to put yourself first? I'd like to imagine that you know that self-care goes far beyond visiting a spa or having drinks at the club. It is not eating your favorite meals or buying yourself the most expensive item on your wish list.

Nah. Don't get me wrong, those things are important too, and of course, they have their place. But self-care runs deeper than that. There's a whole lot more to that process than those superficial things.

It may seem painfully obvious that you need to focus on self-care, but you'd be surprised to realize that you may not know exactly how to look out for numero uno in this kind of situation.

Here are some practical ways to get you started on your self-care journey:

Stop the obsession spiral

If you don't know what I mean, the obsession spiral is when you start to replay all the events that have happened and wonder what went wrong. You'll take a magnifying glass to the fabric of your dissolved marriage and examine every stitch and button. You'll spend precious time poring over those memories and replaying those arguments. Eventually, all these thoughts will coalesce into an intrusive spiral, and you'll soon find that it's the only thing you do.

If this sounds like you, you need to stop immediately. Call yourself out when you notice the spiral and redirect your thoughts. Writing in a journal or discussing with trusted friends will also help.

Anticipate the hard days

I'll admit this is very unusual advice, but I find that preparing oneself for a negative experience helps a lot. So days like birthdays, anniversaries, holidays, and any other special days will be hard. You could find yourself sitting around and thinking. You may feel compelled to call up your ex to share that day with them, or you may try your best even to ignore it.

All these approaches are wrong. Here's what you do. Accept that the day is coming, prepare yourself for the emotions, and schedule a time to wallow. I suggest thirty minutes. Immediately after this time, fix an event that's impossible to cancel. Ask a friend to make sure you attend. It could be taking your kids out, drinks with trusted friends, or even an appointment with a therapist.

That's it. This way, you process the feelings well before the day, and you're not caught unawares.

Choose positive coping mechanisms

Sure, there's nothing wrong with having a huge glass of white wine after the kids have gone to bed or lighting up a joint when they're off with your ex. No judgment here. What I'm concerned about is that these acts may soon become the norm instead of the exception, and we'll have a full-blown addiction on our hands.

I know I sound extreme, but I'd like you to understand that these methods of dealing with the pain will only harm you in the long run. Another poor coping mechanism is throwing yourself into your work. Overworking yourself isn't commendable on any level and should be avoided.

Instead, take up a new hobby, start some exercise routines or spend more time with friends. This will help you cope in a better way, and you'll be healthier and happier at the end of the day.

Give yourself the gift of self-compassion

This simply means forgiving yourself, accepting that going through a divorce isn't the end of the world, and being positive about the future. This is the perfect remedy for the obsession spiral and any other intrusive thought processes you may have.

Even when the situation looks bleak, maybe you're in a lot of debt, and your credit score is shot to hell, don't dwell on criticizing yourself harshly. Instead, forgive yourself. Accept that you're not the only one who's gone through that kind of situation and tell yourself that you'll get through it, just like others.

Ask for what you need

Ask for the support you need. Ask your friends to come over so you can talk to them. Ask your siblings to watch the kids so you can take five minutes to get out of the house. Ask for help with your finances if you're stuck. Ask to see a therapist if you're overwhelmed and confused. Unfortunately, no one will give you what you need if you don't ask. It's simple, in theory, but you can do it, and you should.

Remember that you need to give yourself grace and take your time while putting your future self in perspective. It may shock you to realize that you're a lot closer to your future self than you'd imagined.

Making New Friends

This is a great time to talk about the fact that there has to be a conspiracy afoot. Yeah, a conspiracy. I mean, why is it so hard to make friends when you're older? It's doubly hard even to want to form new friendships when you realize that you lost a few good ones during the divorce.

Then again, if you could 'lose' them to the split, perhaps they were never good friends in the first place. I'll leave you to think about it.

It can be stressful to go out there and meet new people and decide actually to be friends with them. But we can't deny the fact that you need friends. So how can you navigate this without looking like a chump?

As usual, I have some great steps you can take to start making new friends immediately:

1. Call up your old friends.

It's possible that the entire divorce process may have left you unable or unwilling to contact your old friends. Or you've just not felt up to hanging out or having them around. Now that you've decided to socialize more, you can just reach out to your old friends and say hi. They most likely won't hold the breakdown in contact against you because they understand how harrowing a divorce can be. So start from them, apologize for not reaching out and suggest an activity, you both love. This will help you get into the swing of things and prime you to meet new people.

Another great hack to meeting new friends through your old friends is to host a party or event and ask your friends to invite their own friends. If you don't like hosting, you can either ask your friend to organize an event or attend a mutual friend's event together. It doesn't have to be fancy; it could be a movie hangout or attending a concert together. The most important thing is to make sure that you get to connect with people you feel comfortable around. Don't pressure yourself.

2. Get yourself ready to meet new friends

Right. You know that you'd love to meet new people but are you even good enough to be friend material these days? Yes. Yes you are. A few important pointers to help you look, well, friendly and approachable are:

- Be yourself. Don't pretend to be someone else or change parts of yourself that you think are unattractive. The fact is, there's only one you, and you have no choice but to own it. Don't be desperate to make a new friend or be needy. Just be as natural as possible. If it works out, great. If not, that's great too.

- Be open-minded. Meeting new people means experiencing people with different ideals, standards, and values. You're bound to hear or see one or two things you may not like. Don't freak out or cancel them because of it. Most friends don't agree on everything anyway. Just have fun with it and try to find common ground between you.

- Put yourself out there. If you're the shy type, putting yourself out there may be very difficult, but it's entirely doable. Of course, you'll have to leave the house for that physical interaction. Once you're successfully out of the house, you have to take the first step sometimes. Start a conversation, pay someone a compliment or ask a thoughtful question.

- Keep to your promises. We all say, "Let's meet up soon" or "Let's have coffee soon!" Unfortunately, most people don't make concrete plans and flak out on seeing their new friend again. If that sounds like you, you need to stop. If you're genuinely interested in seeing your new friend again, make specific plans and ask if they're okay with it. If you sense they're not as eager to meet again as you are, then ease off and try again with someone else.

3. Go out and meet new people

There are so many creative ways and places to meet new people. Some of them are at your workplace, your kid's school, neighborhood events, or even church. Trying out a new hobby or exercise can also help you meet new people. People with a common interest are quite easy to talk to because you already have something in common, right?

Social media is also great for meeting friends, but you must exercise caution and stay safe.

There you have it. These three power tips will help you find new friends no matter where or who you are. Try it first, and feel free to modify it to fit your circumstances.

Reinventing Yourself

Contrary to popular opinion, reinventing yourself doesn't mean you're changing yourself because of self-hate. It also doesn't mean that you're rejecting your old self and all it stands for. Nope. It's not a violent process or an action borne out of hate or desperation. Rather, it's a natural consequence of your self-compassion, self-love, and self-care.

Spending a lot of time with yourself helps you take stock properly, find the parts of yourself that aren't compatible with your future vision, and naturally shed those parts away. Reinventing yourself comes about as a part of that process. It's a great way to get past the mental state associated with the split and enjoy your life as it is.

The best way to reinvent yourself is to:

Let yourself breathe

Again, there's no pressure propelling you into becoming someone else. Just allow yourself to exist in the knowledge that you've undergone a phase of your life and that you're now in a new one. What are the things that don't sit well with you? Are there things you've always wanted to try, or you've been curious about? This is the perfect time to consider them and see if they'd be a good fit for you.

Don't settle back into old patterns.

We are creatures of habit. This means that despite your best intentions and resolutions, there's a high possibility that you'll slip back into your familiar routines. It may be an unconscious act, or you could just be scared of trying new things and prefer the comfort of the familiar.

Either way, it's important to stay accountable to your goals. We've established that the old ways no longer fit the new you. Mentally remind yourself to stay dedicated to whatever new habit or practice you've taken up. Stay accountable by keeping a trusted friend in the loop. That way, they'll observe you and keep you in check.

Update your looks

Look, hand on heart here, I promise you that you're underestimating the effect of changing your looks. I'm not trying to be vain or cliché, but there's *something* about looking different. The best part is that you don't have to do anything fancy. You don't have to spend a fortune on changing your look. It can be something as little as getting a different haircut, growing your hair, or putting highlights in it. Have you always wanted to try makeup? This is the perfect time. Go wild (not too wild), experiment, and try it. You'll know what I mean when you get into it.

If you were not into exercising and eating healthy before, you might want to start now. Everything about you changes when you take fitness seriously. It's a great way to complement your new changes.

Give yourself permission to be happy again

You may discover that you're more than a little skeptical about ever feeling true happiness again. You may have made up your mind to put yourself out there and maybe date a little, but you're definitely not making any long-term plans. You may not even have consciously decided this, but you've made up your mind that you won't ever get *that* involved with someone else again. Maybe you feel like you don't deserve ever to be happy again, or you're so jaded that you don't believe that true happiness even exists.

You need to take time to examine all these assumptions and find their root causes. You deserve to be happy. You have to let yourself accept this. It's not a simple process. It means watching how you think, studying your instinctive choices, and digging deep to see why you do what you do. At the end of the day, it'll be totally worth it.

Of course, a relationship isn't the only source of happiness, or you may not be ready to face one just yet. That's absolutely fine. As long as you're concerned about your happiness, and you're intentional about it, you're on the right track!

The best part about reinventing yourself is that anything goes! You can do absolutely anything you want, with no limits! Take this time to explore yourself and enjoy falling in love with yourself all over again.

Taking Time to do Things You and Your Child Enjoy

Taking Time To

I get it. Trying to balance your career, handle your finances, sort through the divorce processes that need attention, focus on your healing, have a social life, keep the kids alive and fed, and the list marches on. Even if you don't have primary custody of the kids, spending meaningful time with them could be tough.

But the rub is, you need to stay connected to your kids all the more in this period because this is when they need you the most. How can you get quality time with them and make this time count? How can you feel that connection and closeness you used to feel before?

Here are a few tips to help you get meaningful time in with your little ones:

Find ways to include your kids in your routines

Sometimes you may not have to insert yourself into your children's lives; all you need to do is to include them in your own routines. Are you trying to stay fit? Take them along for your daily walk. Do you want to start reading more? Have a collective reading time in the park or maybe at the back of the house. You could read separate books and discuss them. Look for ways to get them involved in your daily life.

Specifically carve out quality time for them

You may spend a good part of your day in close contact with your kid, but at the end of the day, you may not have spent any meaningful time with them.

To make the most of your time with them, set aside time where you can both sit and talk or do something fun together. You could bake cookies together or make a special snack together. Ensure that you ask them questions about their day, their interests, and their opinions on things. Make this a daily routine, and you'll suddenly find that you know your kid a lot more.

Play games while you're in the car.

If you have a long commute and your children are young, play car games like 'I Spy' and others. You can even involve your older teens in these games so that everyone joins in the fun. You could also make use of the commute time to talk to them as well.

Remove distractions

Your phone, those thoughts in your head, that work document you really want to get through tonight, and even that mental list you've been assembling in your head are all potential sources of distraction that could take away from your quality time with your kid.

Try to limit them as much as possible or take them away entirely if necessary. Remember that they'll only be children once, and you need to experience as much of their childhood as possible!

Ask for help

Asking your kid to help you out with a minor chore or two is a great way for them to feel valued. If possible, ask them to join you while you're doing something. That way, you'll be able to spend quality time with them while you're working.

Your kids need to feel loved, wanted, and cherished as much as possible, and a little goes a long way. If you do practice these tips, you'll find it easier to connect with them and spend more meaningful time with them every day.

Joining Support Groups

I once knew a lady who had endured a horrible divorce from her narcissistic ex-husband. She managed to keep the kids, but only by the skin of her teeth. She had a very demanding job and tried her best to be strong for the kids. As for her, she wasn't sleeping well; she was always tired and worried. She had a lot on her mind, but whenever she tried to discuss it with her family or friends, they never quite seemed to get her. She stumbled on a social media platform that talked about a support group for women who had divorced their narc exes.

She said that it felt like she was home. She could relate with what she read online, connected with a few women, and provided support for others seeking courage to do one or two things.

"I'd always seen myself as a broken woman who was damaged too badly. But being with all those ladies in the support group was beautiful. I felt seen, encouraged, and validated. To my great shame, I used to think that support groups were for people that were mentally weak, but now I know that's not true at all."

A lot of people labor under the misconception that support groups aren't as good as they sound. Some think that people who join or are in support groups have weak minds and are easily controlled. On the contrary, people in support groups have better emotional support than others.

Joining a support group may just help you get the emotional support you need. You'll also get access to valuable advice from people who have been where you are currently and can also help. You could choose to join one such group in the area or search for a platform to help weed them out.

You could also choose to join an online support group. There are many types of support groups, those for women and men, those that address parenting issues, those that focus on romantic life after a divorce, and so forth.

How do you know if you'd benefit from joining a support group? These pointers are helpful:

- If you feel overwhelmed and stressed by the divorce process.

- If you don't have any clear plans for the future post-divorce.

- If you're not coping well and your mental health is affected, you will definitely be affected.

Joining a support group may easily be the answer to all your burning questions, and it's worth a second glance.

You Can Love Again

The concept of love and dating as it applies to you differs from that of someone else. Many factors come into play when you're trying to decide if you'll ever love again or get married one more time.

The biggest factor to consider would have to be your experience with your narcissist ex. What sort of emotional abuse did you suffer? What harmful self-beliefs have you internalized as a result of that experience? Do you still believe in love? Can you ever trust someone with your heart again?

Your kids. How will they handle meeting someone new? What if the person you introduce them to doesn't like them? Or worse, what if your kids don't like your new partner? What if things don't work out with this new partner, and you have to introduce someone new to the kids again?

It's a heavy burden to carry, but at the risk of sounding cliche, yes, you can find love again. But you'll find it when you're not looking for it. Make no mistake, falling in love with someone else after experiencing an abusive marriage worsened by a messy divorce requires a great deal of thought and intentionality. That's a given. If someone who claims to be your true love just fell into your lap, would you accept the love without hesitation, or would you do your due diligence? We all know what the better answer is here.

What I mean when I say that you'll find love when you're not looking for it is that there has to be a process for refining and redefining you.

Rebuilding Your Life

You have to focus on yourself first. You have to basically fall in love with yourself before you can love someone else. You have to learn your own likes and dislikes. You have to learn how to be gentle and cautious without yourself. You have to dig deep to understand any underlying issues you might have.

While doing the mental workout, you should also pay attention to the physical. Eating healthily and working out are great practices for your body. So stay fit and toned, wear sunscreen, and try a new hobby. Focus on yourself and on loving yourself.

Introducing your new partner to the kids can be tricky, but you must first ensure an appreciable degree of permanence in the relationship. You don't want your kids to meet different people who may not be great fits for them. You also need to know that picking someone that likes your kids and is comfortable with them is very important. Prepare your kids before the meeting and ease them gently into spending time with your new partner. As time goes on, they will most likely get to know each other better and like each other. Don't let your partner assume the other parent's role immediately or even at all.

Get the right kind of support or therapy to work on self-healing and be prepared for the next stage. You've made it this far, and you're doing an amazing job. You'll conquer every obstacle you'll encounter along the way, and you'll come out a winner.

Conclusion

What kind of reader are you? Are you the type that doesn't mind skipping to the end of a book if you feel that the book got off to a slow start? Or do you take time to systematically review every chapter and note every section?

If you want to get the full value from this book, I advise reading the entire thing cover to cover first so that you have a broad overview of the content; then, you should re-read parts of the book as you need to. In fact, I'll encourage you to note down the parts of the book that you feel drawn to re-read and plan to do so over the next few days.

If you've made it this far, you're amazing. Trust me; I'm not trying to patronize you or anything. I just want you to recognize that we've come quite a long way from the introduction to this book, and I'm confident that you're much closer to becoming the type of parent that wins at life even though you just got divorced from a narcissist. You may not see it yet but implementing the gems in this book will do a lot more for you than you may expect.

So far, you've accepted that getting over the divorce may take you longer than you may imagine or even want. You've seen that grieving your marriage – mourning the good times, accepting that you were once deeply committed to your ex, wishing that your kids could have a home where both parents are still together – is normal. You now know that

Conclusion

refusing to accept that fact or trying to blatantly ignore it will only retard your healing process. Now you know the possible reasons why moving on from your marriage is hard, and you know the best way to mourn your divorce for you. You've understood the phases of divorce recovery – much like the phases of grief – that you may experience; you know what stage you're in right now and what to expect in the coming stages.

This was probably very difficult for you, but you examined your relationship with your ex to identify the signs of abuse you were unaware of. You've seen how they tried to damage you emotionally and how toxic the relationship was. Maybe you even discovered that you've been having symptoms of PTSD, but you didn't realize it until this book. That's alright because you now know that being intimate with a narcissist can cause PTSD and even Narcissistic Victim Syndrome. Thankfully, we looked at ways to safeguard yourself from your toxic ex after the divorce and how positive psychology can make a huge difference if you let it.

The fact is, surviving a divorce is more than just 'keeping it together for the kids' or avoiding the drama as much as possible. It's about cold, hard facts. Are you in debt after the divorce? Is your credit score poor? How can you get started with fixing your credit score? What are the things to look out for so that you don't get fleeced by your ex in court? Can you try to consolidate debts and make sure you're not left paying for a debt your ex incurred? Which assets should you pick? How does the state you live in affect the splitting of debts and assets? Whew, that's a lot of questions, but I'm sure you can agree that we answered these questions and much more in the book.

Now, you're probably hyper-focused on how to protect your child(ren), and you need to find the best way to break the news of the divorce to your child. You're probably wondering how to tell your five-year-old the news in a way that'll help her understand that both of her parents still love her and that it's not her fault. You also know that telling your ten-year-old boy needs a different approach than the one you used for your five-year-old. We explored all these angles and even looked at the possibility of your child liking your ex more than you or even outright hating you. We looked at the best way to decide if your child needs therapy and what to do next if it's needed. Co-parenting may not work with a narc ex, so what do you do then? Well, I'm sure you're not confused anymore because you've learnt about parallel parenting and when to practice it.

I think learning about positive parenting is a turning point for everyone, and I'm curious to know if it was for you too. Feel free to leave a comment about this on Amazon or send me an email with your thoughts. I'd love to hear them.

We started this book with a focus on you, and it's only fitting that it ended with a focus on you as well. I'm proud that you've come this far and learned so much. I know I'm flogging a dead horse here, but I hope you don't forget to give yourself grace. I hope when you look up, you'll see a survivor who's lived through emotional abuse and more, who's learned to heal from the encounter and nurture themselves. I hope you see yourself as that parent who's a steady anchor of love and understanding for your child(ren) and as an individual who deserves a second chance at love again.

If you've enjoyed this book, please leave a comment and a review so that other awesome folks like you can be encouraged to get it and change their lives too.

References

Seay A, Freysteinson WM, McFarlane J. Positive parenting. Nurs Forum. 2014 Jul-Sep;49(3):200-8. doi: 10.1111/nuf.12093. Epub 2014 Jun 5. PMID: 24898152.

Luthar SS, Ciciolla L. What it feels like to be a mother: Variations by children's developmental stages. Dev Psychol. 2016 Jan;52(1):143-54. doi: 10.1037/dev0000062. Epub 2015 Oct 26. PMID: 26501727; PMCID: PMC4695277.

Joussemet, M., Landry, R., & Koestner, R. (2008). A self-determination theory perspective on parenting. Canadian Psychology, 49(3),194-200.

Joussemet, Mireille & Landry, Renée & Koestner, Richard. (2008). A Self-Determination Theory Perspective on Parenting. Canadian Psychology/Psychologie canadienne. 49. 194-200. 10.1037/a0012754.

Duineveld, J., Parker, P., Ryan, R., Ciarrochi, J., & Salmela-Aro, K. (2017). The link between perceived maternal and paternal autonomy support and adolescent well-being across three major educational transitions. Developmental Psychology, 53(10), 1978-1994.

Juffer F., Bakermans-Kranenburg M. & Van IJzendoorn M. (2008). Promoting positive parenting: An attachment-based intervention. New York: U.S.A.: Lawrence Erlbaum/Taylor & Francis.

Sandler, I., Ingram, A., Wolchik, S., Tein, J., & Winslow, E. (2015). Long-term effects of parenting-focused preventive interventions to promote resilience of children and adolescents. Child Development Perspectives, 9(3), 164–171.

Kumpfer, K. L., and Alvarado, R. (1998). Effective family strengthening interventions. Juvenile Justice Bulletin. Washington, DC: Office of Juvenile Justice and Delinquency Prevention. Retrieved from https://www.strengtheningfamiliesprogram.org/about.html

Masten AS, Barnes AJ. Resilience in Children: Developmental Perspectives. Children (Basel). 2018 Jul 17;5(7):98. doi: 10.3390/children5070098. PMID: 30018217; PMCID: PMC6069421.D'Onofrio BM. Consequences of Separation/Divorce for Children.

In: Tremblay RE, Boivin M, Peters RDeV, eds. Emery RE, topic ed. Encyclopedia on Early Childhood Development [online]. https://www.child-encyclopedia.com/divorce-and-separation/according-experts/consequences-separationdivorce-children. Published: June 2011. Accessed November 25, 2022.

Potter, Daniel. (2010).Psychosocial Well-Being and the Relationship Between Divorce and Children's Academic Achievement.

Journal of Marriage and Family. 72. 933 - 946. 10.1111/j.1741-3737.2010.00740.x.Parental alienation can be emotional child abuse - NCSC. NCSC. (n.d.).

Retrieved November 26, 2022, from https://www.ncsc.org/__data/assets/pdf_file/0014/42152/parental_alienation_Lewis.pdf

Wallerstein, Judith & Lewis, Julia. (2014). Disparate parenting and step-parenting with siblings in the post-divorce family: Report from a 10-year longitudinal study.

Journal of Family Studies. 13. 224-235. 10.5172/jfs.327.13.2.224.Nguyen-Feng, V. N., Sundstrom, M., Asplund, A., & Hodgdon, H. (2020, March).

Bringing attention to childhood emotional abuse in psychotherapy with adults. [Web article]. Retrieved from https://societyforpsychotherapy.org/bringing-attention-to-childhood-emotional-abuse-in-psychotherapy-with-adults

Child maltreatment (2017)Administration for Children and families. (n.d.). Retrieved November 22, 2022, from https://www.acf.hhs.gov/sites/default/files/documents/cb/cm2017.pdf

References

Aknin, L. B., Norton, M. I., & Dunn, E. W. (2009)From wealth to well-being? Money matters, but less than people think. The Journal of Positive Psychology, 4, 523-527.

Bremner JD (2006). Traumatic stress: effects on the brain.Dialogues Clin Neurosci. 2006;8(4):445-61. Doi: 10.31887/DCNS.2006.8.4/jbremner.PMID: 17290802; PMCID: PMC3181836.

Dunn, E. W., Aknin, L. B., & Norton, M. I. (2008). Spending money on others promotes happiness. Science, 319, 1687-1688.

Fredrickson, B. L., Tugade, M. M., Waugh, C. E., & Larkin, G. R. (2003). What good are positive emotions in a crisis? A prospective study of resilience and emotions following the terrorist attacks on the United States on September 11th, 2001.Journal of personality and social psychology, 84(2), 365.

Gable, S. L., & Haidt, J. (2005). What (and Why) is Positive Psychology? Review of General Psychology, 9(2), 103–110.https://doi.org/10.1037/1089-2680.9.2.103

Howell, R. T., & Hill, G. (2009). The mediators of experiential purchases: Determining the impact of psychological needs satisfaction and social comparison.The Journal of Positive Psychology, 4, 511–522.

Kashdan, T. B., Uswatte, G., & Julian, T. (2006). Gratitude and hedonic and eudaimonic well-being in Vietnam war veterans.Behaviour Research and Therapy, 44(2), 177-199.

Płonka, Agnieszka. (2019). An assault on the individual: a preliminary comparative study between the psychology of a socialist state and narcissistic abuse. 10.13140/RG.2.2.17812.86409.

Peterson, C. (2008). What is positive psychology, and what is it not? Psychology Today. Retrieved from https://www.psychologytoday.com/us/blog/the-good-life/200805/what-is-positive-psychology-and-what-is-it-not

Scott, B. A., & Barnes, C. M. (2011).A multilevel field investigation of emotional labor, affect, work withdrawal, and gender. Academy of Management Journal, 54, 116-136.

Shulamith Albeck & Dania Kaydar PhD (2002).Divorced Mothers.Journal of Divorce & Remarriage, 36:3-4, 111-138, DOI: 10.1300/J087v36n03_07

Vernon, L. L., Dillon, J. M., & Steiner, A. R. W. (2009). Proactive coping, gratitude, and post-traumatic stress disorder in college women. Anxiety, Stress & Coping, 22(1), 117–127.

Vickie Howard (2019) Recognising Narcissistic Abuse and the Implications for Mental Health Nursing Practice, Issues in Mental Health Nursing, 40:8, 644-654, DOI: 10.1080/01612840.2019.159048

Scott, S. B., Rhoades, G. K., Stanley, S. M., Allen, E. S., & Markman, H. J. (2013). Reasons for Divorce and Recollections of Premarital Intervention: Implications for Improving Relationship Education. Couple & family psychology, 2(2), 131. https://doi.org/10.1037/a0032025

Hawkins AJ, Willoughby BJ, Doherty WJ. Reasons for divorce and openness to marital reconciliation. Journal of Divorce & Remarriage. 2012;53(6):453–463. doi: 10.1080/10502556.2012.682898.

Clarke-Stewart, A., & Brentano, C. (2006). Divorce: Causes and consequences. Yale Univ. Press.

Lucas RE. (2005 Dec.16)Time does not heal all wounds. Psychol Sci. (12):945-50. doi: 10.1111/j.1467-9280.2005.01642.x. PMID: 16313658.

Reporter, D. M. (2010, April 7). How long will it take to get over divorce? 17 months and 26 days to be precise. Daily Mail Online. Retrieved November 8, 2022, from https://www.dailymail.co.uk/femail/article-1264157/How-long-divorce-17-months-26-days-precise.html

Aacfl. (2022, January 13). Impact of divorce on the finances of men, women, and children. AACFL. Retrieved November 9, 2022, from https://aacfl.org/impact-of-divorce-on-the-finances-of-men-women-and-children?doing_wp_cron=1667993975.7694840431213378906250

Hauser, R., Burkhauser, R. V., Couch, K. A., & Bayaz-Ozturk, G. (2018). Wife or Frau, women still do worse: A comparison of men and women in the United States and Germany after union dissolutions in the 1990s and 2000s. In M. Erlingagen, K. Hank, & M. Kreyenfeld (Eds.), Innovation und Wissenstransfer in der empirischen Sozial- und Verhaltensforschung (pp. 167–188). Frankfurt/Main, New York:

References

Campus.de Vaus,

D. A., Gray, M., Qu, L., & Stanton, D. (2017). The economic consequences of divorce in six OECD countries. Australian Journal of Social Issues, 52(2), 180–199. htttps://doi.org/10.1002/ajs4.13.

Made in the USA
Las Vegas, NV
03 August 2023